Narcissism 2021

Learn everything you have to know

Introduction

Human psychology is a complex problem. People enjoy various character traits that can be traced based on their life experiences and genetic origin. Every day, the psychologist tries to understand the reasons why people do what they do. Over the years, many modules have been developed that show the reasons for human actions. For many, however, personality remains a great secret: narcissism. Narcissism is a personality that many people have seen over the years. Although there are theories that try to explain why people exhibit narcissistic behavior, nothing seems to stop this problem. To understand the issue of narcissistic abuse, we must first go back to the basics and understand narcissism itself. We need to understand more deeply what narcissism is, what it does, and how it happens. Studies have shown how much misinformation abounds in narcissism. Public perception of matter is a hotbed of ideas that do not match and are too simplistic, with a contrasting sense of what is "healthy" self-improvement and what is not. Much of the inappropriate rhetoric published online takes a black and white approach as if narcissism was a pure and direct "label," not a series of healthy and unhealthy reactions and behaviors caused by 98% of people (including you). It is very likely. These behaviors occur at different intensities for different periods. Results depend not only on basic mental processes, seemingly persistent but on what is happening in life at this moment (and recently), which can aggravate generally inactive problems with self-esteem. Narcissism exists in the spectrum from low to high levels. Some narcissism is healthy, and some of our typical responses to our ego threat, which allows us to preserve our sense of identity without suffering shame and failure. At the top of the scale are a personality disorder known as a narcissistic personality disorder (NPD), characterized by an arrogant sense of superiority, an overstated sense of importance, and a deep need for admiration

What is narcissism?

The word narcissism comes from the ancient Greek myth of Narcissus, a young man who was deceived by a ghost to fall in love with his reflection. He became so obsessive that he eventually starved. Unfortunately, Narcissus never realized that he was in love with meditation and not a real person. He died trying to achieve perfection. But the tragedy does not end there. There is a less known character in the myth called Echo, a nymph with a unique curse: he could only repeat what others had told him. He could not share his thoughts and feelings. One day he saw Narcissus walking through the forest and immediately fell in love with her beauty. Although he tried to get his attention, his curse prevented him from communicating. Narcissus only heard the echo of his own words. Echo's story also ends with despair. Finally, she died of a broken heart. The story of Echo is known to anyone who has had a relationship with a narcissist. You try to reveal yourself, but your efforts seem doomed to failure. You rarely (if ever) feel seen or understood. Your perspective is ignored, and your feelings are annulled. Like weak Eco, your communication attempts fail. Sometimes you feel invisible, angry, depressed, and humiliated. You will close yourself in the fight for recognition. While the narcissus looks with lust in the mirror, you look with desire at the narcissus. But unlike the simplicity of the Greek myth, relationships with narcissi in the real world alternate between ups and downs. Unfortunately, you repeatedly experience ecstasy and despair Echo when the link changes between periods of idealization and devaluation. What exactly is narcissism? The term has a long and dark history. One hundred years ago, it was used to describe the form of male sexual perversion. Since then, the word narcissism has meant many things, including a phase of psychological development, a way of establishing relationships with others, a form of self-esteem regulation, a character trait or style, and a personality disorder. Today, narcissism is the term most commonly used in the context of narcissistic personality disorder (NPD). Personality disorders are characterized by permanent personality traits that cause problems in life and interpersonal relationships. In the case of NPD, these problematic personality traits revolve around the issue of self-esteem. Unlike more concentrated ailments like phobias or panic attacks, personality disorders generally affect many areas of life. Personality disorders may require long-term treatment and may cause complications such as depression, anxiety, and substance abuse. Recent studies analyzing the results in the famous narcissistic test, Narcissistic Personality Inventory (NPI), suggest that unhealthy narcissistic features can be divided into three dimensions: eloquent, selfish, and vain. This book is organized using these three categories as guides.

What causes narcissism?

Looking at statistics, the number of about one percent of the population with narcissistic personality disorder seems unbelievably high, perhaps uncomfortable. For now, we've created a broader and stronger idea of who is usually interested in him. As we can see, narcissistic personality disorder certainly does not discriminate, although some criteria increase the likelihood of this disorder occurring in humans and appear to be more common in men than women. Although we look at people who have a narcissistic personality disorder, or rather groups that appear to represent most of their disorders, we have not yet investigated a large number of root causes. The main purpose of this chapter will be to analyze the various causes of narcissistic personality disorder and what might lead someone to develop this terrible disorder. The exact causes of narcissistic personality disorder are currently unknown. There are many indirect hypotheses about what causes them, and they all culminate in the general modern vision of what leads to the development of this disorder. The current consensus regarding the development of narcissistic personality disorder is that it is ultimately a combination of genetic, social, environmental, and biological factors. The exact role of each of them in the development of this disorder may vary from person to person, and the exact subtype of the developed disorder may vary equally. This means that there is no certain combination of causes that lead to the development of one specific subtype. Immerse yourself in the big question, "why is this happening?" What's more, let's see one by one to get a more solid understanding of the causes of narcissistic personality disorder. First, let's look at the genetic aspect: there is a lot of evidence that the disorder itself can be inherited. The existence of a family member with the disorder is more likely to develop the disorder by themselves. Duplicate studies were beneficial enough to show that the disorder had a hereditary appearance. However, it can be difficult to determine how much this is because a person is growing up with someone who has a disorder, for example, if someone's father had a narcissistic personality disorder. This would undoubtedly lead the child to assimilate this impact and, to some extent, be affected by the disorder, and it is more likely that there are several environmental factors besides genetic factors. Here, we will analyze social and environmental catalysts for the development of narcissistic personality disorder. They are thought to play an important role in the development of the disorder, which is greater than genetic or biological causes, although the environment and biology are likely to play equal roles, or that the environment has little effect on biology. One of the main catalysts for the development of narcissistic personality disorder is that the child learns the manipulative behavior of his parents or friends. Manipulative parents are prevalent, and, unfortunately, manipulative parenting styles have not been condemned for a long time. Developmental psychology and emotional abuse become problems widely discussed in the second half of the 20th century, as a result of which there are still quite old parenting styles that are extremely unhealthy. What's more, it's not just parenthood; it also depends on the person's overall lifestyle. It's a pity, but because of the way manipulative behavior works, a manipulative person can surround himself with people who can manipulate and never have to change their behavior. For this reason, they could teach him a child as a norm. With the growth attitude of children who change dramatically in the 21st century, this problem is expected to become less and less important when people discuss issues such as mental and emotional violence and become more acceptable vocal themes. Until then, it will be a fairly important catalyst. This is accompanied by another catalyst for the development of narcissistic personality disorder: emotional abuse in childhood. Manipulative behavior and emotional violence are not necessarily the same, but often go hand in hand. In the latter case, a narcissistic personality disorder may develop as a defense mechanism or defense mechanism. They can be one of the most difficult cases to treat from a psychological point of view because remedying those means facing a much deeper trauma. This is comparable to trying to force people to rationalize their position in other people who did not have to endure emotional abuse as a child. This does not mean, however, that narcissus developed it as a defense or defense mechanism. Many people develop the disorder because of things that happen to them in other ways. For example, many people like to write that there is not much praise for the child. However, as the child develops, many of the actions presented to him, if he stands out in any way, will be intensely shaped and settled in his brain forever, unless they make a very active attempt to unlearn him if someone is too much praised. , may develop the view that nothing can be done wrong. Often this happens with single parents who do not want to lose respect or adoration for their children, unfortunately and have seen that it appears in many such cases. Similarly, if a child is overly criticized, he or she may develop a narcissistic personality disorder as a defense mechanism. If people are constantly telling someone that they are extremely beautiful or talented, with little foundation in reality or poor realistic and earthly opinions in response to praise, there is a risk of developing a narcissistic personality disorder. If people overestimate or like them too often, they are more likely to develop the disorder. The mind wants some balance in terms of interaction with other people. Do everything possible to achieve this balance and search for it. Believe it or not, but not all minds are equally resilient and can easily resist certain tensions or excesses in life. In other words, many causes of narcissistic personality disorder can be seen as excess parenthood. Someone who praises, criticizes, or over manipulates a child exposes you to the development of a narcissistic personality disorder. Narcissistic parents often use their children as a means of self-determination and impose their narcissistic behavior on their children. This generally leads to the unwillingness or development of the Stockholm syndrome. In the first case, people can terminate contact with parents or limit contact as much as possible. In the latter case, they will often be modeled after their parents. As for the biological factors that correspond to the development of this disorder, there is not much research to be developed. As I said before, finding finite opportunities to study narcissistic personality disorder can be difficult. However, studies have shown that the areas of the brain dealing with empathy, emotions, and compassion are generally not as large as those of neurotic or non-psychotic people. One of the questions that many people may ask when reading this is whether they can know if their child is narcissistic or not. If you've collected this book before because you are worried that your child is suffering from this disorder, then I have a relatively disappointing answer for you: your hypothesis is as good as mine. The point is that, although one of the things associated with the development of narcissistic personality disorder is too sensitive as a child, it is one of the few signs that can be seen in the development of narcissistic personality disorder until reaching puberty. Many hypersensitive children are not growing up because of this disorder. This means that we are a bit lost in terms of the specific response. If you are concerned that your child is a narcissist, check his parenting style, and learn about his family history. If other people show signs of narcissistic personality disorder or if you tend to praise your child excessively without realistic comments or excessive criticism, you may have a narcissist in your hands. However, many children and adolescents will show the symptoms of narcissism as a transitional phase before they eventually abandon it. Their brains are maturing and have a lot to learn about the world. Depending on how young they are, it is enough to approach their age wisely. If you are anxious or if your child has an excessive number of symptoms, planning a trip to a child psychiatrist for professional assessment may not be a bad idea. If you find you suffer from narcissism or a related mental disorder, your psychiatrist will work with you and your child to find a way forward.

Who is the narcissus?

A person who has a narcissistic personality disorder is generally dissatisfied. These people are very gentle and can become brutal if they do not get the attention they need. They ask for everything they deserve and try to achieve it through manipulation and strength. Many people can view narcissistic individuals only as selfish and loving. Narcissism, however, has much deeper roots than selfishness. Narcissism requires someone to take what he thinks should be his, in every possible way. Narcissistic people do not pay much attention to the feelings and desires of other people. Their needs and personality are a priority. They get what they want, regardless of being stepped on someone on their way. Although there are therapeutic options for narcissism, the biggest problem is patient acceptance. Narcissistic people may not think they are suffering from this disease. Even people close to him may not recognize a person suffering from narcissism. In cases where friends or family know the symptoms of narcissism, a narcissistic person needs to seek help. Many of them think that they are better and better than anyone else. Narcissism can be easily detected. Because this condition causes more harm to family and friends than to the person who suffers from it, everyone should be aware of the symptoms. Early detection of narcissistic behavior can help avoid offensive relationships or help a narcissistic person get help.

The next thing we need to analyze is some signs that the person you are with is narcissistic. Many narcissists do well at work and hide well who they are. It takes them some time to look at them and capture small things, and maybe even have close relationships with them before they discover they are narcissistic, or also before they notice that something is wrong with their way of acting. When you spend time reviewing the general definitions given by Narcissus or NPD, it's easy to draw conclusions and assume that anyone who looks unpleasant or someone who has used the manipulation only once is enough to call it narcissistic. While we will all talk about manipulation and perceive it as something negative, we all use manipulation in one way or another. Therefore, we need to spend some time analyzing what would classify this person as a narcissist. According to the information in the American Psychiatric Society Diagnostic Manual, a person classified as narcissistic will have at least five features that we will discuss below. Narcissus exaggerates with a sense of importance.

People who consider themselves narcissists and have NPDs will love others who find them truly better. Although it's good to have the idea of being better when you are, most of the time, the narcissist will not have the results or the ability to justify these feelings. They will think that their skills are much better than they are, and therefore they will try to devalue the skills and all other contributions that others make in every situation. You'll often find that the narcissus thinks that everyone he meets should be able to appreciate him. And when they do not receive this kind of praise, the compliments that they deserve for some reason will be surprised and annoying. So, if the narcissus does not receive such recognition and success, which he seems to have, it's time to blame the people around him. This fault can be transferred to the whole society, another person, or situation. The responsibility is never on the narcissus's side, even if the narcissist thinks they are unusual and unique. There is nothing wrong with the right level of self-esteem and confidence in life in the world in which we live; these can be perfect things. But when we look at someone narcissistic, they are more likely to take him to the extreme. They often think that they are so unique and special that only other exceptional people can understand them. Therefore, narcissus wants to surround himself only with the best and can include doctors who see and friends with whom they associate. For example, if the narcissus is subjected to some therapy, it will be specified how it wants to be perceived only by the best person.

They do not want to go to the first open therapist; they don't want to work with someone who is a student and learns. They want to be sure that only the best can work with them. Narcissus will feel that you have to admire him all the time. Most of the time, the narcissus will act with excessive confidence and will be very proud of this process. But even after that, their level of self-esteem will be quite low, which makes them fragile. Narcissus will have a high tendency to worry about how others perceive them. So when they learn that the people around them are not prone to worship and admiration, the narcissus will be shocked and hurt, and he will show his disgust. This is something that appears very much to the narcissist. Narcissus will come in and behave as if he loved the other person with whom he was in a relationship, but it will only last as long as the worship of the other person lasts for the narcissus. Narcissus will look charming and may even fill the other person with feelings and attention (in a process known as love-bombing), but when a couple tries to defend themselves or try to protect themselves, everything disappears. We must remember that the narcissus will expect others to admire and want to be like them. So when others come back or have a different opinion, it will cause some problems. Narcissus, in such situations, will become very angry and can be frightening, and in some cases, can also become abusive. Narcissus feels good.

When we see a narcissus, we'll find that they often feel empowered to do things they don't have the right to. These narcissists will appear in the false belief that existing rules and laws are not for them and apply only to others. There are several methods that a narcissist can use to present this, including disrespect for others, which should guarantee much higher respect. This can be seen when the narcissus is angry and dismissive of any authoritarian figure. You will also find that the narcissus will be waiting for the others to lean and jump over the wheels so that they can fit in. And when someone does all this, the narcissist will not appreciate anything that has brought him hard work. When we look into the mind of a narcissist, they see that it is perfectly reasonable for him to change his life around them and even plan events and more around him. So if they choose him, they won't also appear, despite all the hard work. They think they can do it, and everyone else should accept it and not feel nervous or disturbed in any way. Narcissus fights with every form of empathy for others. Many times the narcissus will be known because he will not be able to understand or understand the pain, struggles, or emotions of others. There are times when this person will seem perfectly reasonable and rational. But then they will say something that is incredibly insensitive, having no idea why it offends others and makes them do it.

Narcissus is very jealous. Many narcissists like to compare themselves and their lives with other people. And often, they will not choose their neighbors or friends, but those who are successful and famous. Doing so will be even worse for the narcissist because it will increase their jealousy. And if they manage to succeed in life, they will happily believe that others are also jealous or jealous of them. Narcissus is often arrogant and arrogant. Think about the time when you were on a date with another person, and at that time they could easily choose the best quality wine from the list, it was sweet and delicious for you, and it seemed like the perfect catch, just for them to be wrong and rude to the server? It is often a sign that we should be careful about an incorrect date, and it can also be a sign that a person is narcissistic in combination with some of the other symptoms we are talking about. Narcissus will be like this and even manage to remove him from the restaurant. They will behave as if they were an arrogant snob, someone who knows everything and can never be mistaken about anything, so everyone else is ignorant and can be diminished. If you start noticing these qualities with someone you spend time with, that person will most likely be a narcissist. Narcissi will devote time to successful fantasies and will find the perfect combination. Often, a narcissist spends a lot of time thinking about how to gain the respect of others, success, and excellent strength. They are even happier if there are three things from influential people. It's something that will play an essential role in many parts of your life, including how you choose the person you sometimes want to have a romantic relationship with. Some research has been done on this topic and helps us see how narcissists attach the highest importance to such things as physical attractiveness and status, rather than observing any other characteristics and personality of such a person or nice. Narcissus will not worry about these next features. The reason for this is that the narcissist thinks that when his partner looks good, he can help him raise his image and make the narcissist feel better. Narcissus often uses others. When you combine the lack of empathy and the law that narcissus entails, you'll find that it's easy for them to take advantage of those around them without feeling bad. And they will do it to anyone and as often as they want, provided they provide the narcissist with some benefit along the way. Because the narcissist believes that he has the right to get what he wants and behave the way he wants and that they do not care or understand how others will feel, they will go ahead and use every person they want.

This is one of the reasons why it is difficult to work for someone narcissistic or someone with NPD. If you work with a narcissistic boss, they will try to help you with fieldwork and can often confess to the work you have done without feeling bad, giving you the compensation that you should do for it or provide you with respect, even narcissists outside the workplace can use you. Many times it will be a different kind of friendship or relationship in which a person is not afraid of getting angry or trying to do what he wants. It would be like that friend who is always too busy to spend time with you until you find something they want. You know that they fall apart all the time, but they keep coming back and trying to use you. Many different features appear when we look at someone who may be a narcissist. Someone who exhibits one or two of these characteristics is sometimes not as important. But when a person shows these features regularly and shows five or more of them, we can be quite sure that this person is a narcissist and, above all, we will worry about the benefits and promote them, not paying attention to what will benefit and support your partner.

Different types of daffodils and how to detect them

Narcissism manifests itself in many different ways, so there are many types of narcissus. You can classify narcissi based on how they work in relationships or based on the features they most often manifest. In this chapter, we will see the five best types of narcissus. If you spend a lot of time with a narcissistic person, you can show characters that belong to more than one category that we will talk about in this chapter, but if you want to find out which category a particular narcissist belongs to, always go with the one that covers your most characteristic features. Dominant. Here are the five main types of narcissus you'll probably meet at some point in your life:

Junkie

When a narcissus uses a person, it is not always the victim's fault. This is because everyone can be deceived and become an emotional victim; In short, everyone is sensitive and a target for toxic types. It is essential to know the characteristics that narcissists are looking for to be able to protect themselves and to be able to avoid them. And this is when he reaches the point where the future victim knows that he is being exploited or attacked. Their qualities are known to be great when allowed to use them positively.

For an evil narcissist, their characteristics will dominate, but unfortunately, they will use it against another person.

Psychopath

Sadistic type. This type of narcissus is often confused with psychopaths and people who have other antisocial personality disorder. They do not regret and are not interested in any moral or immoral behavior. His self-esteem is arrogant and overpriced. They feel that they have to make fun of other people. They are mainly gangsters in prison or a drug rehabilitation center. They are known for humiliating others through unusual sexual fetishes.

Exhibitionist

They are the least sensitive, but the safest. They think they are better and will always seek revenge or be angry with people who treat them disrespectfully or dare to negative comments. This group has no sense of shame and has a high level of self-esteem. They result from the superiority they gained at the time when their parents made them feel better than their childhood. Unlike sensitive narcissists, they act only as expected from childhood.

They don't care how others perceive them, and they can quickly leave the conversation if they don't get the admiration or respect they deserve. If they are in a relationship, they don't care how their partners perceive, and they can quickly leave the link if they don't get the recognition they deserve. They will openly have many relationships and will not be proud of how people look at them and how great they are. They can be very dominant and very aggressive when analyzing problems.

Persecutor

These narcissists act on the assumption that one is built by shattering or humiliating the other. Intimidation is intended to confirm your superiority, and this kind of narcissus is ruthless in the way he does it. We're not talking about the stalker in the schoolyard: the narcissistic stalker is much more sophisticated (although his methods may be somewhat similar to the ways of the stalker in the schoolyard). This type of narcissus treats others with contempt, hoping that they will feel losers, letting them feel victorious. It is a person who will look down on you at every step, bring out and pour cold water into all your efforts to improve. Your criticism is never constructive: they aim to make fun of you and say that it is unable or deserving of improvement. When this kind of narcissist wants something from you, he doesn't ask for it. He asks for it; As if it was something you need.

Seducer

They are narcissists who tend to manipulate people in their favor. Unlike other narcissists, they can really make you feel good about yourself, but this feeling doesn't last long: it ends as soon as they get what they want. Seduction will begin to express admiration for you, but it is always something they think they want to hear, and the point is that they offer them the same appreciation so that they can use you. When seducers get what they want from you, they reveal their true colors and pull the rug under their feet. Such a person can still offer compliments, but when he fulfills his request, they begin to turn their backs on him. If you're dealing with a person who is always flattering, try to see if he does the same with everyone else. If kindness is directed only towards you, the reason may be that they indicate manipulation.

Emotional manipulation is one of the red flags or characteristic features of how narcissistic violence can be. Narcissus will use language in some way to blame a partner or other person for challenging his feelings or reality and giving him the feeling that you are the culprit, not the narcissist. In a sense, narcissistic bullying is a way of controlling thoughts because of how they use language to stimulate guilt, regret, paranoia, doubt, and other mental/emotional states. Abuse is a form of psychological and emotional manipulation that causes the victim of abuse to question his wishes, thoughts, personal autonomy, and much more to achieve the narcissist's priorities and intentions. Here's how you can look in life when you are a victim of narcissistic bullying: you can challenge your mental health. You may find that you don't trust people who support you in life, such as family and friends. You may feel convinced that only a narcissus cares for you and loves you, and that everyone else has abandoned you. Feelings of worthlessness refuse to recognize any hard work, knowing that only your narcissistic partner discredits you. He has doubts about whether he can make the right decisions or think clearly and effectively. Complete the disconnection of personal desires and needs. Whatever you want, do what you can to gain the favor of your narcissistic partner by controlling your thoughts and beliefs about yourself. Having obsessive thoughts about any failure or mistake that you think you made, Devalue has regular contributions. He lives in denial of narcissus, apologizing for his behavior. Idealize your narcissistic partner, who mentally "trained" you to do so. Having obsessive thoughts on how to make them happy. These situations do not always occur and these are symptoms of narcissus' mental and emotional manipulation. It turns out that it manifests itself in this way and can be very subtle and happen for a long time, even before you can recognize that you are being harassed and emotionally manipulated. Let's create an example of how it could look in everyday life. Let's say that the victim of narcissistic bullying appears at the first therapeutic sessions and feels uncomfortable, in a state of uncertainty, emotional stress, and disconnection from his true feelings. Today she is here because her partner showed her that she has problems and needs help if she wants to remain in society. He could present himself in a way that seems to be an obsession about his failures and failures, talking about his flaws and the desperate need to heal his problems and failures that his partner told him. It may also happen that she did not properly meet the needs of her partner and did not meet her expectations, which means that he is not present enough for him, is too attentive to children, and excludes him or does not have enough have fun sex. The victim is constantly worried about trying to understand why she was not able to please her partner and why she still tells her that she does not understand why she still fails to meet her expectations. He has no idea that he sets it on fire and creates a reality in which he must doubt himself to survive. You can also ask him why he is unhappy or unsure; at this point, he tells her that she is unhappy and insecure and that he makes fun of him, convincing her that he has a problem, not him. During the therapy session, the victim may begin to reveal comments of hatred, condemnation, and self-image, as well as an image of his worthless person who has never been a good companion and wants only to understand how to make her happy. This may include defensive statements eliminating the partner from guilt, another symbol of the power of narcissists, and control over the partner's mind. Statements may include some of the following:

We take a lot of time, I like it a lot, and we laugh a little. I'm just a handful of small things. There are no big problems. I know it's all my fault and only I have to change. Can you help me settle down so that I can be a better partner? Help me understand how I can disturb you constantly. I can't lose it, so I have to find out how to fix it. I know it's all my fault, so how can you start loving me? Do you think there is hope for improvement? Such repetitive statements or cycles, and thought patterns are just the tips of the iceberg, how psychological and emotional violence are manifested. It's a long and difficult journey of constant manipulation and emotional abuse that can distort your mind in the belief that you have to blame someone's personality disorder. Here are some other examples of how these types of narcissistic tactics of violence can manifest themselves in sacrifice: the word 'failure' is often used to describe their inability to support a partner. (For example, I can't make him feel more loved or more secure). You can't "learn" how to fix or improve it so you can stop hurting or annoying your partner. He can do nothing to cause more difficulties, for example, call him to shout at him, interrogate him, punish him, etc. He is not entitled to blame him for any of his problems. She is confused as to how she could be so nervous or so "crushed" by "small things" that they should not matter so much. If you oppose your partner's request or set a limit, it is called "crazy," and it is suggested that you may need the help of a professional or that you should take medication. He could accuse himself of being the reason or reason why he decides to have problems during his relationship and wants to know what he can do to fix himself, so he stops. The victim believes what the narcissist told him: it's his fault if things are what they are in the relationship, and she needs to fix and improve. Emotional violence is how the narcissus keeps his partner in a state of mind that will allow him to continue as he does in his relationship to life and how they maintain a relationship with the partner in a long-term relationship. It is not always aggressive, threatening or offensive, but it has the basis for suggestibility and manipulation as a subtle and strategic goal of convincing the victim that he is not brave and is not able to do so many things to keep him in a worse position and mental state, in some In severe cases of narcissistic abuse, symptoms may manifest as post-traumatic stress disorder or post-traumatic stress disorder. Some of these symptoms may include but are not limited to, Stimulating thoughts and memories that appear out of nowhere. Emotional and physical reminders of traumatic or offensive moments. Awakening experience in your mind or night dreams. Negative, sad, and negative thoughts about you or the world. Surprise or easy surprise Irritability Becoming overly watchful obsessive compulsions Challenges related to the concentration of insomnia Detachment or a sense of isolation from other people in your life The pattern usually begins with a tornado, a bombarded love story that seems unbelievable and allows it to reach full speed, even eyes in love with your partner, and show no signs of his manipulative nature at the beginning of the journey of love. There is an important reason for this: the narcissus does not want you to know that he will treat you differently later, and most likely, he will not even know it. He has not yet reached the stage of the relationship in which he no longer meets the needs of the deities of love and narcissus, so at first, there are no significant signs that emotional violence is hiding around the corner. It may take weeks, months, or even a year before you realize that you are not old at all, or at least who you were when you fell in love with them for the first time. Your friends may even notice that you have changed and acted as if you were not yourself, and then convinced them of what your narcissistic partner convinced you: "We are amazing to each other because we are very good at fighting, and then we come up with. We're so in love, and I can't see my life without him. He likes things in a certain way. Who can blame him? When you enter the hideout of emotional abuse, your excuses accumulate, and you ultimately believe everything your partner has told you and do all the work necessary to convince everyone around you that you are happy and cooperating. Make your life happy. Narcissus repeatedly shows you how to think, feel and act around them, and you begin to understand that everything they say or think about you must be true, even if it means hating each other and doubting the process. Here's how emotional abuse works. Unexpectedly, he falls into sarcastic comments or comments. It seems public, embarrassing, and embarrassing in front of others, while your partner is relieved to be better. He replaces any internal trust and knowledge he may have and turns his self-esteem into doubt and an inability to reflect on his life and situation. Narcissus has power over you and can control your mind, will, and personal beliefs about yourself and the world through emotional tactics. Here are other examples of how narcissistic they can be: Verbal abuse Sabotage Blocking and delaying Refusal to help or help as a form of punishment Toxic level of projection (causing unwanted feelings or emotions to another person) Triangulation (refusing to speak directly to you but you talk to another person, to communicate, forming a triangle Intentionally harmful blows and counterattacks In the cycle of abuse it is quite difficult to accurately determine what is happening to you or what is being abused. A narcissistic attacker has extensive experience in shooting situations, events, and realities that belong to their needs and satisfaction, and can keep you in the space of abuse by committing love bombs and bouts of sweetness after aggressive action or an argument to convince the victim that is not abusive. They can even use tactics to convince you that you are abusing it.

The following symptoms are one of the most common side effects of experiences related to emotional violence. Your partner does not have to be narcissistic for this to happen. However, the tactics of psychological manipulation used by the narcissist are often associated with these symptoms. You disconnect to survive. Dissociation is about dividing or separating from something. In situations of emotional abuse, it may be necessary to separate yourself from the environment completely. This kind of attachment can affect your sense of identity and sense of self, your perception of reality, your memory, and your consciousness. It is a way to fall asleep from the trauma of bullying. The feeling of mental numbness to survive a situation may consist of repeating pointless activities, addiction, and natural obsession with certain things or events. In this way, you can escape from the reality in which you live. In this way, your mind can block anything that can be emotionally harmful or painful so that you don't have to deal with the full facts and truths about the reality of your relationship. Dissociation is a common factor in an abuse scenario. The aspect that allows them to exist or survive in the current fact is how many people learn who they are and what they want after a long time to maintain this reality in a particular society. Walk on eggshells. In a traumatic situation, regardless of whether it is traumatic or not, the goal is to avoid reliving or recreating one of these traumas. Narcissistic bullying is traumatic, even when it seems subtle and challenging to detect. When you are afraid to touch the nest of a wasp or wake up a sleeping bear, you can "walk on the eggshells." It can only mean that you are too cautious in all your actions or anything you can say to avoid anger or unpleasant attitudes and behaviors of your partner. In general, walking on eggshells is not a solution to the narcissist's problem, because you will probably find flaws or misunderstandings about their behavior and find a way to feel worse. Walking on eggshells probably also applies to your relationships and activities outside this association, and you will have difficulty getting pleasure and appreciating the world around you because you are always careful and careful not to disturb anyone or anyone,

Ignore and sacrifice physical, emotional, and basic needs for the sake of the perpetrator. Regardless of how you got used to meeting your needs, you may have noticed in your relationship, or under the influence of narcissistic bullying that all you do is make sure your partner is happy and that it can be a full-time job., You may have felt the opposite at the beginning of your relationship (love bombardment phase), but when you become more united and deeply involved, you become a guardian and to please your partner, you sacrificed all your time and energy to ensure that all your needs will be met, often by your sacrifice. This can increase over time and lead to an emotional crisis, pain or physical symptoms, and even minor problems due to the neglect of basic health needs. Narcissus will never be delighted, no matter how well he satisfies his needs, so the tragic loss of himself when he gives everything he has. Health and psychological problems. By supporting the crucial last point, your dedication will lead to more severe problems over time. Lack of self-care to please another person will lead to deep agony, which will begin to manifest itself physically, mentally, or emotionally or both! Your physical health can get worse when you are not in the right balance with yourself, and you can get sick more often or even develop chronic problems that don't go away no matter how many times you get help from your doctor. This can usually be a good indicator that your physical illness is related to something more psychic.

Mental problems also often occur in states of abuse and may include depression, insomnia, anxiety, paranoia, obsessive disorder, mental and emotional fatigue, and more. You may be wondering where these problems came from since you've never had such issues before. Of course, the last person he would accuse was his attacker. This is where cycles and bullying patterns are stuck in repetition. You must honestly ask yourself why you have health and mental problems. The culprit is probably narcissistic abuse. Generalized lack of trust gaslighting is a common tactic of the narcissistic aggressor. Gaslighting mentally manipulates someone to question his mental health. By experimenting with him repeatedly, it is difficult for him to trust someone, especially his perpetrator. Because you are slowly and continuously "learning" to question mental health or mental health, it will be difficult for you to trust another person and their statements. He will even lose the ability to trust himself, believing that his thoughts and experiences must be invalid or false.

There are thoughts or tendencies to self-harm, and the pain of violence, whether it happens or not, can cause an endless cycle of depression, anxiety, and despair. These circumstances can become unbearable over time and as if there is no hope of getting out of pain or the current situation. It is possible that his attacker convinced him by subtle and subversive means that he is vulnerable and will not be able to save him if he tries. This kind of thinking pattern creates the need to escape, change feelings through self-harm or self-harm, and can even lead to suicidal thoughts. Isolation Sometimes, a narcissistic partner will create a situation that isolates them both so that they find themselves in their little world so that they cannot be disturbed or interrogated. In some other cases, the victim of abuse will be isolated, usually because of shame or feelings. Not being able to escape or explain the terms of the association, it's easier to separate than to seek help and find solutions. Withdrawing from others seems to be the safest option, especially after the perpetrator convinces you that you are not mentally healthy, and you should not trust your instincts. Fear of success and do what you want. Narcissists often envy others, including their partners or victims of violence. You can get something extraordinary in your life to feel the punishment of your attacker. A narcissistic attacker mentally conditions his partner or victim that he will feel his success negatively and consider it a problem, not something to be proud of. This will lead to depression, anxiety, lack of self-esteem, lack of self-confidence, and many other symptoms. Under conditions of bullying, it will be almost impossible for you to prosper and do what you love.

Protect your offender and be enlightened when the models are established, and you are in a "comfortable" relationship between the offender and the victim, you'll feel compelled to rationalize your relationship and experiment to minimize problems and deny it for any reason. Concern for their relationship. It's usually about saying that everything you did to provoke a partner was your fault and that you should have known better. It is also easy for abusers to demand their love in moments of spell and reconciliation in order not to lose it. This maneuver supports the offensive cycle and gives a narcissistic advantage. All these situations can fall into the gravitational spectrum, which depends on the relationship. Not all narcissistic accounts will have such an intense or severe form of psychological and emotional violence. If you are reading this chapter and feel that your partner may be bullying you, it's time to start identifying problems that you can change or ask for help. It is unlikely that you will change the narcissist's actions and behavior, so it's up to you to be ready to stay in such a toxic situation.

An intense traumatological bond arises between the rapist and the victim. This is because the perpetrator "prepares" the victim for life in this way, and the victim chooses to remain a survival tactic. In a traumatological relationship, the victim will be jointly responsible for the abuse and even blamed. Do you blame yourself for the dramas of relationships? Is your partner responsible for your problems or actions? What should I do now? If you have a relationship that is used in any way, don't be afraid; You are not alone, no matter how lonely you feel. Many people are harassed who can understand what is happening or what happened. Seeking help begins with recognizing problems. The first step is to raise awareness of your situation and the reality you have been in and to confirm your feelings and experiences. Your attacker may try to manipulate your thoughts and ideas or give you gas, but you still need to recognize the problem if you want to get away from cycles and patterns of bullying and heal the wounds he caused. If you're not ready to face your partner about what you think is going on in your relationship, start writing it all down. Take a notebook or diary with you and track any accidents or experiences you may have. Compare this information with some of the narcissistic signs and symptoms of bullying that you read in this book.

If you can, find a therapist or clinical social worker who you can trust and share your truth. Tell some family members what is happening in your relationship. Talk to friends and loved ones who are inexperienced and can offer perspective. In your experience log, you can start processing your feelings and identify systems and abuse cycles created by your partner. You can also try other forms of treatment, especially if you're dealing with physical or mental health symptoms. Abandoning this kind of relationship can be very difficult, especially if traumatic relationships arise. There are many reasons why people do not want to leave their partners, even if there are cycles of abuse. However, an essential part of all this and the reason you read this book is learning to heal and help you lead a healthy and prosperous life, even if you have fallen victim to narcissistic abuse or have had a relationship with a narcissist. You may also have children to consider and desire the best for your happiness and health. In the next section, you will find more information about the influence of a narcissistic parent on children. Perhaps you were also the son of a narcissist, so that this chapter may contain alternative types of information.

Idealization

Idealization occurs when a narcissist or attacker puts you on a pedestal. He tells you how wonderful you are that he can't live without you and how important you are to him. This stage usually involves a lot of presents for you and is associated with an emotional level. You feel loved, appreciated, and desirable, and you live with that feeling. It's a stage you can't wait for. It keeps you also connected during the other four phases, and even less so. It means a whirlwind of romance, seduction, love, praise, and worship. This stage is often associated with promises about the future, such as marriage, buying a home, or children. The pledges made here are designed to attract your desires and make you want to stay in a relationship. In this phase, you want to feel desirable and become addicted to feelings. Think about a wedding: this is the wedding stage. That's when everything seems to see and live in a new light. If you have already gone through this cycle, the idealization stage is full of fear because you know what to expect. Although you like to feel that they love you, you also see the danger if you somehow offend your partner. You understand that the devaluation phase will occur if you do even the slightest evil and try to avoid it at all costs. Do everything possible to stay good, thanks to your partner.

For example, imagine a marriage, Anna and Eric. Eric is a narcissist. In this phase, Eric sings all praises to Anna. He invites her, gives her jewelry, and buys her a new phone because she knows her phone is faulty. He is attentive, tender, and seems to be the perfect companion. Anna raves about this phase of the relationship, flourishing with love, and believes that this time it could be different. He does what he can to be a loving wife, making sure her clothes are ready; dinner is prepared and makes sure that she has close intimacy with him. He understands that his personality is sometimes explosive, so he tries to avoid disturbing him or doing anything that may irritate him. Over time, passion and romance seem to fade away. Although they can still interact regularly, and it's mostly positive, the continuous floods of love are beginning to fade away, providing a healthy relationship. Anna doesn't care because she knows that passion decreases and increases during the link.

Devaluate

In the devaluation phase, abuse begins to return to the relationship. Return to it as it was as if nothing had changed. You can start with verbal abuse when your partner yells at you for small mistakes that are not a big problem in the big scheme of things—even buying the wrong butter, which costs $ 0.39 more, maybe enough to make your partner feel annoyed. Your partner may accuse you of deliberately catching this butter, even if you just took the first stack from that particular sign. He accuses you of wanting to fight. So you can see gaslighting, which aims to convince him that he is wrong about the perception of events. He may fool you again if cheating was one of the problems in your relationship, or he could bet or drink more than you agree. During this phase, your partner wants you to be quiet as tension increases. Silence is acceptance of the narcissist and, if necessary, will work with it. He wants to teach you to accept abuse and calm; that is to say, you do it when it comes to narcissus. During this phase, you are in a position where you can intensify your actions even more by calling a narcissus for every abuse you encounter, or you can be silent. None of these options are particularly good, but ultimately you must keep your limits. At this stage, you can defend yourself, and if you feel disrespected, it is permissible to leave, temporarily or permanently. In the case of Anna and Eric, Anna could see that Eric's clothes smell of perfume again and that she physically likes her less. He continually accuses her of being sticky or needy if she tells him that she wants to spend time with him, and also starts calling her if she frustrates him. Even if she hasn't done anything wrong, she finds a way to blame her for her bad mood. He could have left the stove for too long and overheated, or maybe he forgot to wash the shirt he knew he was wearing every Friday. No matter what you come up with, you'll have something to choose from.

Waste

Then comes the rejection phase. This usually happens if you refuse to consent to abuse. If you call the narcissus for his behavior, asking for treatment with respect or hoping that you will not be cheated, he will most likely be offended. Remember that the worst thing a narcissist can ever imagine is to reject altogether, ignore, and reject, so that's what he does to you. Thinking that you act the same way he does, he decides to get rid of you in the hope that he will teach him a lesson. The waste phase often requires some silent treatment or abandonment. It may break up with you or refuse to recognize your existence. He believes that by not tolerating his bullying, you respected him, even if his bullying was disrespectful of you, and defending borders is something to be expected. After all, in an affair, they don't cheat on you or say names. You had the right to defend your borders and refuse to abuse narcissists. During this phase, Anna could tell Eric that she was aware of the adventure she was experiencing.

You can see that he saw the messages on his phone or found the hair of a second woman in clothes while washing, as well as lipstick spots on the neck of this shirt, for which he insisted that he not wash when he appeared wonderfully this weekend. He points to the evidence and calls him, claiming that he disagrees with the treatment and infidelity that Eric responds by grabbing the keys, coat, and telephone and walking away. He reads the news when he writes to him, judging by the small "READ" notification at the bottom of everyone, but he never responds. It is tranquil. Hours become days, and he refuses to communicate with his wife. At this point, he begins to worry but does not recognize his existence. She knows she is at work every day, but every time he is connected to his office line, he disconnects from her. This stage is to make Anna feel weak as if she didn't care. She tries to tell her that if she doesn't like it, it doesn't matter and she'll throw her away like rubbish. After all, the rejection phase ends, and the relationship revolves around destruction or aspiration, depending on what you do. If Anna does not continue to object, the link will likely become empty. If he continues to name his behavior, he will most likely take steps to destroy.

Destroy

If the rejection period ends with a conflict, or if you are still trying to summon a narcissus to behave, the next stage is the destruction stage. Then everything will explode. Narcissus has an explosion, and violence is escalating even more. It can become physical or sexual or may involve threats. Either way, this stage is meant to tear you apart emotionally and most likely physically to surrender. Narcissus will intensify its behavior by choosing typical methods of use and will not stop. He will do everything possible to hurt you because he wants to make you suffer from the pain he seems to have caused him. He feels so offended that he wants to hurt you just like him, even if he sees himself as a victim because of a distorted perception of reality. This is reason enough to justify his actions. During this abuse, you are likely to isolate it by keeping it physically locked somewhere or removing keys, telephone, money, or anything else you can call. This stage concerned a narcissist who insisted that he should control him. He misses his partner and blames her. This stage is by far the worst in terms of damage done during the abuse cycle. It is explosive, dangerous and can end in someone's death if it is allowed to continue or if the narcissist decides not to stop. This is the most critical part of the relationship, mainly if the narcissus usually uses physical violence. Not everyone will do it, but those who do it are particularly dangerous during this period.

For help, He wants to make sure you're stuck and wants to leave you to think about what happened and how it was your fault. Eric could return home with Anna after an extended stay with his partner. He came to show her that he could come and go as he pleases and that nothing Anna would say would be enough to convince him otherwise. When he tells her, he ends the relationship if he does not finish things and challenges him and his actions by physically attacking her. It affects her, something she has never done before. Although it does not spoil anything or cause permanent damage, it leaves traces on it. He tries to call the phone for help and decides to pick it up and crush it, saying he bought it as his own and does what he wants. After a long punishment, he takes the keys and leaves her alone in the room with a brief commentary on how he provoked her.

Vacuum cleaner

The stage of aspiration takes its name from emptiness, referring to the fact that the narcissist will try to absorb it. He knows that he has severely damaged the relationship, and especially if he sees that you are not trying to save the link, he will try to do it instead. During this phase, he will decide to reject the guilt for the attack. He will blame you or some other external cause. He may say that he was sick, stressed, or under the influence of drugs and alcohol, and therefore thinks he cannot be blamed. At this point, it is a sacrifice, and nothing else matters. He may say that he is very sorry and promises to do it better. He'll probably cry and tell you that you are the best he has ever had and that he can't believe he ruined him. The critical thing to remember is that you don't want to say anything about it during this. He says everything he needs to do to save him and bring him back online. He does not feel bad about what he has done and wants to make sure that he is ready to maintain a relationship with him. You may not want to deal with divorce advertising, or you want to avoid moving or losing children, but for whatever reason, you desperately want to deal with it. At this point, there will probably be signs of an apology: a luxurious gift, a candid letter (but not because the narcissist doesn't like it) to apologize, and even do something for you that you wouldn't normally do. He wants you to think that he is doing everything in his power to agree to continue the relationship. Eric can come and apologize to Anna, offering him a new phone since he destroyed the older man in anger.

You can see that this time he got an improved model, and if he wants, he offers a takeaway dinner at his favorite restaurant for dinner. At this stage, he is ready to do what he wants and tests the water to make sure he wants to stay. If he says he's leaving, chances are he won't defend himself now, but cry and ask for forgiveness. He promises to go to therapy, improve, and end his relationship with another woman. Sure, it's all a lie, but expect him to say it convincingly enough for Anna to believe it. After a while, he may decide to try again, assuming he will go to therapy and that his relationship will end. He says he will go away the next time he is having an affair and may agree that this seems reasonable enough.

After achieving aspirations, the relationship returns to the stage of idealization. You have heard again that everything is perfect in your relationship and that everything will be fine, but you cannot but feel that you know that your partner can do what he has done. You are worried that you will be able to attack again and although you enjoy the moment you have now, you cannot relax. During this phase, the narcissus usually behaves, at least for a while, and fulfills what he promised. He doesn't cheat you, hurt you, scream, or do everything he has promised not to do. However, this never lasts. As before, you will eventually do something or blame something, and the relationship will return to the devaluation phase in response to the threat. The cycles can take weeks, months, or even years, or they can be done almost every day. Ultimately, there is no clear guide on how often someone can sway during a bullying cycle. However, it is clear that abuse almost always returns and practically always increases to be worse than before. Ultimately, the choice is yours if you decide to stay in the abuse cycle or choose to leave. Remember that there are resources that will help people living in fear of abuse or being actively abused. You can go such a relationship if you want, and you can find support groups of survivors of such violence. Remember that if you ever feel physically threatened or injured, you can and should call 911. They can help you get rid of this cycle if you allow it.

Gaslighting Narcissist

One of the things that makes narcissism fascinating and frightening is the difficulty of knowing exactly what makes them work and what their specific motivations and goals are. We generally know that one of the main reasons for narcissus in his life is to get recognition and recognition from others, but what happens on a small scale with a single victim? Sometimes it seems that narcissus destroys a person's emotional health just for fun or to see how far he can go—thinking about sickness and depression. But what else can motivate a person to treat another person like that? Maybe we can get a little closer by looking at some of the basic features of a narcissistic personality. We have already discussed the general lack of empathy that applies in all areas to different narcissistic subtypes. But there is another critical aspect of the narcissus, which is the only thing he tries to hide more than anything else, and this is uncertainty. It is important to remember that people are not born narcissistic, personality is formed due to many different factors related to nature and care, which are too complex and unusual to be able to materialize on a worldwide scale. However, when looking at the narcissist's history, one can sometimes hypothesize that the aspect of his education/childhood/adolescence could have contributed to his final transformation into a narcissist. One of the reasons why it is so important to determine why narcissus is so is the apparent lack of sense and lack of purpose associated with the use of emotionally manipulative tactics, such as igniting gas in another person. What exactly is gaslighting, and how does it affect the victim over time? Primarily, gaslighting is a manipulative process that, over time, prompts the victim to question various aspects of his reality. To better understand what I mean, let's take a look at some of the warning signs that someone is burning it with gas.

The biggest and most obvious sign is that a person tells blatant and shameless lies. They can look into your face and lie that you can or may not be sure it is not valid. There is a legitimate reason for the narcissist's confidence in himself and this tactic, and he probably acted earlier. He'll lie to you until you wonder if you know what's going on or not. People who have enough confidence to lie like narcissists will be very effective at releasing them. It will be complicated to thwart their claims because they seem very confident and what they claim to be true. Another warning sign appears when narcissists begin to deny that they even said something when it is known that they did it. It has been said that if you feel the need to record a conversation at any time during a relationship, you should be careful because it is a good sign that you are getting gas. A light gas narcissus will also use things and people that are valuable to you and turn them into emotional weapons against you. They can support their claims about you and your flaws with legitimate arguments, perhaps presenting them in a practical way that everyone knows about it except you. When they manage to convince you that something is wrong with you, as they say, they will consume you over time, using other flaws or convincing you to isolate themselves from other family members or friends, including your children. This can be extremely frustrating for a victim in a gaslight because the words of the author often do not match the person's actions. He will tell you things that can lift your spirits and encourage you. But then his behavior may contradict what he said to you, making you feel that his words are meaningless, and maybe you are doing something that does not respect what he says. Let's look at Claire, for example. Perhaps after a few conversations, the narcissist, let's call him Mark, sees that Claire is more and more attracted to him. He carefully constructed his story and talked to accurately present who he wanted to see, even if it is not authentic. Let's say your relationship is growing, and he can convince her that there are a few things she should work on. Perhaps he mentions something about his personality that he heard the comment of one of his friends.

Mark begins to plant seeds of uncertainty, doubt, and confusion based on things he appreciates. He can promise her the world, and then it seems that she will completely disappear until she asks him to come back with her. So take this opportunity to discover a weakness, to tell her that she would be much happier with her if she solved this or that, maybe her appearance, work or something else. Gaslighting comes into play when he begins to feed his lies and confuses them with things that are contrary to his behavior. Whenever she tries to call him, she responds with high confidence and conviction, informing her that she is wrong. The key here is that over time he will take small steps in this direction. It is slow-burning, and Claire suddenly finds himself buried in his confusion before realizing what is happening. Things I was sure would disappear and connect with the reality Mark wanted to design for her.

The trap is crafty and can last for years or even decades. The narcissistic expert knows that the more they confuse you, the more control they can have on you. They work to make you emotionally sensitive so that you feel you need him to lead you. Mark can take steps to turn Claire's closest friends against her and then blame them for all the emotional turmoil he goes through. At this point, Clair has acquired psychological addiction and feels that she is nothing without Mark. The fall that broke the window and the sign of the narcissus' success would convince you that you are crazy, that you have no idea what you are talking about when you try to condemn him for his lies or his behavior. When they manage to close it and ultimately ask what is going on around you, they will have full control over you. They may want to stop the farce and shoot you further, or they may be bored and decide to take on an entirely new challenge because they have conquered you. If Claire finally understood what they had done to her, she might wonder why? What did he do to deserve this? For any victim of narcissistic abuse, this is a question you'll probably have to deal with. After all, depending on how far the injury has taken place, the victim will have very low self-esteem and self-confidence because she was emotionally beaten to feel useless and stupid. What is the answer to the ardent question? Why me?

I love bombs and devaluation

Another prevalent manipulation tactic that narcissists love is the love bomb and the devaluation cycle. This cycle is primarily about flooding the goal with lots of love, feelings, worship, attention, gifts, and everything else that you think will appreciate your goal. Wet her goal in everything that makes her feel good to create a kind of addiction for her. He grows up to associate her with good feelings of receiving gifts, compassion, compliments, and everything else that plagues him and therefore joins her faster than one might expect. This allows you to speed up the relationship, moving much quicker than a healthy relationship could develop. The exchange "I love you" begins earlier, and the goal so engulfed the vortex of romance that he fell in love with him. This is the love-bombing phase. Love bombs eventually get worse, become exaggerated, and so frequent that they become rational target expectations. When the narcissist is convinced that the target has been captured, the tactics change. Suddenly, he rejects him completely. He decides to kick the pedestal, which he has placed so carefully above, watching him desperately try to return. Suddenly, he is surprised by contempt, disrespect, dislike, and unloving, and he is so dependent on a narcissist that he is ready to do everything in his power to recover it. He looks after everything he asks to regain his excellent favors so that the bombing of love begins again. He wants you to be happy because when she is happy, he is happy. He misses his presence and his love. This gives the narcissus a hefty dose of narcissistic supply in which he delights and restores the cycle. The cycle begins with longer phases of love bombardment and shorter periods of devaluation but slowly begins to lean toward more extended periods of depreciation as well as shorter devaluations and abuses until the relationship turns into almost permanent reduction. At this point, the narcissus probably completely rejects the target.

Reflection and projection

The reflex refers to the tendency of the narcissus to wear a mask. I'm trying to reflect my goals in myself, so to speak, making it seem more desirable. People usually want people like them, and the narcissist is aware of it to some extent. Create a person, a mask to mask your true self from other people, and this person continually changes along with the comments of others. If you had the misfortune to attract the narcissus' attention, you probably introduced yourself precisely the way you want. He will like what he wants, use the means to build relationships between you, and suddenly share the same goals he has, even if he has no idea what he is talking about. He pretends to be the other person in the hope of interest because when he is interested, he can start the love bomb phase to manipulate him further. This behavior has three different purposes for the narcissist. Narcissus lacks a real sense of self because he never developed it, and adopting the personality of another person is a way to create a false identity. Imitation also allows a narcissist to imitate someone who has what he wants. If you resemble the behavior of another person, you are more likely to get the same results as that other person. Finally, imitating others is as close to legitimate empathy as possible. The best thing you can do is not being able to establish authentic relationships and imitate another person. The projection is accompanied by reflection, but it turns around: while consideration implies the thought of another person in a narcissus, the narcissus is reflected in other people during the projection. Usually, this is done to project your faults onto others, trying to deal with the errors and mistakes. He often expects his flaws because they are too difficult to control or because his flaws do not feed his disappointments in size. He can also project his positive qualities if it suits the narrative, makes everyone believe, even he. The most straightforward example of projection to see usually appears when looking at the relationship between a narcissistic father and child.

Narcissus chooses to idealize or create a scapegoat for his children. The idealized have become the golden children of the narcissus, which means they can't be wrong. Golden children are considered perfect and worthy, and the narcissus presents his achievements and praise. They are treated with the same respect that a narcissist thinks he deserves it. Even when a golden child does something that others consider a problem, a narcissist can still glorify this behavior.

On the other hand, the scapegoat is the one who receives the negative side of the narcissus's personality. If the narcissus is not sure that he is not intelligent, the scapegoat will always be capable, even if he is, in fact, the best in his class at school. If the narcissist cares about ugliness, he will always be irritated by the scapegoat's appearance, even if the scapegoat is conventionally attractive. Everything the scapegoat does is automatically considered insufficient and is often rejected and diminished, which minimizes any success. In both cases, the daffodil considers the golden boy and scapegoat to be more than just an extension of himself: none can be their people. Each attempt is canceled as soon as possible.

Play the victim

As discussed briefly above, narcissus loves to play with the victim. It is a tool par excellence that sensitive narcissists use to get compassion or compassion to get what they want. Narcissus has identified what he wants, and the easiest way to achieve this is through guilt. He will try to ask what he wants, and when he is denied the opportunity to get him, he will probably change things so that he becomes a victim. Usually, by dismissive comments about yourself, that the other person feels guilty for causing such feelings, the narcissist knows that he can use the other person's ability to prove what he wants, exactly what the narcissist wants. ,

FOG

Another acronym, FOG, means fear, commitment, and guilt. Narcissists love to lose their victims in the fog in their relationships. Just like when you try to walk the roads in the mist, and you realize that you can't do enough to drive safely, narcissists make sure that you do not see enough in your relationship to notice the dazzling red flags flying around, the fog is so dense, that the flags disappear. In situations where you are afraid, you will most likely do what you need to make sure you are not injured. After all, we are so scared when we are at risk of damage or death. It is a way to tell him that he is currently in danger and to tell him that he should do everything to stay safe. Sometimes keeping safe means listening to what the narcissist likes to convince him to protect. Duty motivates him to do the right things for the people he loves or is loyal to him. Narcissus takes advantage of this by making you fall in love with her, so you feel responsible for looking after her or considering her feelings about matters that affect us. You want to see her happy and healthy and feel a particular obligation to do it for love, maybe because she has done something for you that she can't afford. Narcissus will use it in his favor, fulfilling his obligations whenever he seems to resist and therefore feels guilty. It is liable to deny the narcissus everything he wants and feel a sense of guilt if it means he is more likely to give up. You can blame yourself for any adverse consequences, such as saying that it is your fault if she is injured or if her children are hurt because of their inaction. If he deceives you, he can make you feel guilty by saying that you shouldn't have made her feel so lonely, blaming her for not paying attention to the decision to pay attention elsewhere. Usually, this is the last effort to keep you online, because maintenance and commissioning require a lot more energy. Narcissus is needed to hold something that may dominate you, to keep him on the Internet, which can be difficult in specific contexts of relationship. Sometimes it seems that there is a risk of disappearing or deleting them at will, or it may be threatening to release him if he does not obey. While narcissus can avoid guilt or consequence at the top, reaping the benefits as much as everyone else suffers. You can do it in a way that pushes your mistakes to other people, blames the other person, and causes chaos that hides their participation.

For example, imagine a person at work who made a grave mistake. Is it part of a team of people? You can whisper to person A that person B is guilty and show all the ways person B did her harm. You can indicate that person B is having difficulty completing his work as agreed and generally avoids him from other people and underlines all the work he needs to do now. Person A can decide to help the narcissist with his workload by believing that person B is useless. Narcissus would then go to person B and say the same thing as person A. He would complain that person A had given him more work because of the incompetence of person A and discussed how person A thinks he is much better than everyone. Others and is beyond this simple work. Person B, who feels terrible for a narcissist, needs something more than the work of a narcissist while helping himself with reluctance to person A. People A and B blame each other for all problems and additional workload, not realizing that Il narcissus he dropped more work on them.

Lying

When dealing with gas lighting, narcissists do not feel bad. They lie if they think that this is the only way to get what they want. They have no problem telling people what they want to hear if they use it. Especially when trying to bring someone back to the Internet, the narcissist may feel willing to make promises that he does not intend to keep to make sure that the other person returns to complacency. Imagine, for example, someone who just cheated on her husband. Narcissus can cry and promise that he will never do it again, asking her husband for forgiveness. She promises that she will do it better and try to work on herself, and her husband will eventually believe her. He trusts her because most people are honest enough about what they will do to correct the mistake. When people regret something, they often do what they have to do to fix their problems. Narcissus says this only to keep his goal happy. He doesn't care about the pain she inflicted because she cannot have significant empathy. Instead, he promises and holds his promise for a short time before returning sometime later in his old ways. The cycle keeps repeating, with increasingly quick turns, until the target accepts more or less normal behavior and stops fighting it.

Triangulation

Triangulation means deliberately creating conflicts between other people, while a narcissist manipulates the situation behind the scenes to get what he wants. Create a kind of triangle, whispering to other people's ears, telling conflicting stories in the hope of convincing them that the other person is a problem. This causes a conflict between two people manipulated by the narcissus, which then completes the triangle. Two people are arguing with each other

Degrading

Narcissi love to humiliate those around them, both secretly and openly. By humiliating others, they can systematically and effectively destroy the self-esteem of everyone around them. So that they can easily manipulate selected goals because their self-esteem will deteriorate so much that it's hard for them to resist. Narcissists already have a self-esteem deficit. They feel better when they are surrounded by something that they do not have. Narcissus can rely on calling names, disregarding comments, talking about results, refusing congratulations, highlighting failures, or cruel and critical in destroying another person. Over time, after repeatedly hearing that he is unable to do significant work or get a promotion, he eventually internalizes her. Narcissus's words become the words he uses to speak to himself while making decisions and spending the day. If the narcissus has installed negativity in you, this will be your default. Imagine, for example, that narcissus has repeatedly said that you are not beautiful. Note that you never do anything right or that you don't care how it is. He may mean that you are lucky enough to be polite and forgiving or that you will be lonely forever. He could point out that he lacks a kitchen, has difficulties with catching up homework, earns less than an average person of his age in a given field of work, his feet are too large, the size of his clothes is too large, and your hair has the wrong color. It can give you all this for some time until you are so insecure that you can't stop making decisions. After all, you are not smart enough or strong enough, or even insufficiently desirable to make these decisions yourself, and you came to accept and believe.

Quiet treatment

Since the only thing narcissists want more than anything else is to attract attention and admire, they ultimately fear that they will be ignored above all. According to the narcissus, the worst that can happen is not death or harm, but everyone must ignore it and reject it, regardless of what you are trying to do. With this in mind, the narcissist believes that his most harmful and effective method of punishing others is to ignore them. For some people, this is worrying, especially if they had a long-term relationship with a narcissist or if the narcissus is a father or other close relative. The thought that this person is phantoms can be frightening. You never know why a narcissus did what he did, and maybe even refuse to talk to you for a long time, which includes days, weeks, months or even years, before he decides to honor him with his presence.

Intimidation and threats

As expected, narcissists sometimes resort to threats or intimidation to keep people online. Because sometimes the only way to force someone to do something is to be afraid of the consequences of their omission, the narcissus has no problem threatening or intimidating him. It can threaten with taking children, ruining your reputation, sleeping with your best friend, accusing you of beating or bullying her, and even physical threat if needed. You can choose to use signs of aggression, such as throwing a glass over your head or knocking on the door to explain that you are on the brink of physical violence without even putting your hand in it. I could take another step and involve him if he managed to escape in some way. Often, the line between the illegal and the annoying varies and is also told that he overthinks if he tries to highlight it. Intimidation and threats are designed to make you feel that the best option is to stay in a relationship without creating waves or causing the scene because you are afraid of the consequences.

Most of us who have studied and read this subject for some time have noticed that there are similarities in the types of narcissistic victims we choose. Narcissists know that strong, loving, and confident people, with well-defined and clearly defined boundaries, will not tolerate their nonsense. That is why they are looking for people who seem to have a weak sense of self, a strong sense of social responsibility and generosity of spirit, or who seem very willing to please others and treat them honestly and ethically. They can also choose deeply compassionate victims, and therefore do not want to easily give up relationships, even those that are extremely toxic. Empaths are absolutely the perfect candidate for the next narcissus sacrifice. By their very nature, empaths are programmed to fix people and difficult situations, and generally to improve everything for everyone. So, despite their wickedness and judgments about spiritualism, fairies, unicorns, and hippies who believe in them, narcissists love nothing but the awareness of the light that sees the best in the world, and the fighting tigers likely prove that in every there is a spark of goodness. So while the average empath looks at the narcissus and thinks, "Don't worry, whatever you do and what you say, I see God in you. I believe in you, and I know that one day you will do it too, "the average narcissus just thinks," Mmm, lunch! "What narcissists love from empaths, in addition to the incredibly large amount of energy they usually transmit, is that they will forgive them indefinitely and repeatedly for outbursts of anger, gaslighting, sabotage and general culture of tension, darkness, disapproval, and anxiety that generate around us regularly. It is important to remember that many empaths are also healers and, as such, do not want to admit or accept that everyone can be immobile. In addition to self-love and L. self-help, another of the great lessons that empaths are often forced to learn through a narcissist's mess is the fact that as much as we feel and as much as we love someone and believe in his Buddhahood, not everything can be cured with Reiki, song and healing the soul, at least not in one lifetime. Narcissists know that their empathy can be minimal. All they have to do is speak in a way that gives the empathy a bit of hope that may, perhaps, be on the verge of spiritual awakening. If the plan works, the empathy may begin to believe, despite what they have learned from their previous experiences that everything they have always dreamed of was possible with sufficient love, attention, and pink quartz finally comes true. Narcissus, of course, will smile ironically as soon as the emphasis leaves the room to find this wonderful book on shamanism. The empathize smiles happily and finally lets out the air, imagining that the narcissist will wait with bated breath to enter the world of spiritual discoveries, only to find him in a coat and prepare for an unexpected meeting or training day that they insist, that they would mention it earlier. They were swollen with empathic psychic energy and connected by a dazzling variety of agreements and attachments that would empathy. They feed them the rest of the day, marching triumphantly to conquer the world. Remember, when we think about something, we send you energy, and for a few hours after the narcissus leaves the building, empathy will feed them, focusing on transforming every nuance of conversation in their mind, sending waves after waves. Mental energy. After vigorously addicted empathy from false hope, the narcissist knows that life energy will surround them with a warm glow of energy for the rest of the day. Oh, I didn't realize I was dating. Why don't you ever tell me when you are going to leave so that I can plan my time correctly? Why does everything have to look like this at the last minute? I wonder if it works. I'm sure you didn't mention it before you

.Maybe he mentioned it, but he didn't pay attention. No, he certainly didn't mention it. So why would you say you did it if you didn't? However, he seemed interested in the idea of soul recovery. We would have a good discussion about it. I'm the same. Wow, what should I do now? I'm so tired all of a sudden. I can't do much in two hours. It's just not a big enough window! Why is my time always so interrupted? Why can't I do anything anymore? Why can't you have a permanent job? Ugh!! Why am I so exhausted all of a sudden? Okay, I knew it would be hard today because it's your half-day, so whatever you do will be a nice bonus. Let's use this day to survive. Why am I always so tired? It's ridiculous. Even today, I did nothing. I wonder if he is interested in singing with me. Did he mean, or did he say it? Maybe it's changing. I don't know why now????? I'm still going to the weekend. I still need time to reflect. Nothing makes sense anymore. I'm going to take a nap. I need a nap. No, it's chocolate, I need chocolate. I lost count, how many times I went through this scenario. Then, an hour and thirty minutes later, a few minutes later, my phone will ring and Edward will come home and call to ask if I want something from the supermarket, maybe good chocolate or chips .And Edward liked routine. I hated it when everything changed, even a little bit. He knew this because changing routines was one of the things he was most angry at. So I tried to make sure I always answer the phone when I expect it. If I did not, there would be no serious problems, but it would be noticed, and a few days later, I would try to call him for something trivial, and there would be no answer. I have always saved things. Anyway, I said yes to chocolate. Without it, I didn't see how I spend the whole afternoon. My life was full of such small and friendly routines. I didn't live in a golden cage but in a chocolate one. And because he was always out of stock, I always wanted chocolate all the time. And Edward somehow always knew what he wanted. Maybe because he was so good at generating needs. That is why narcissus enjoys and fully utilizes the infinite kindness of empathy and his strong conviction that everyone, cruel or destroyed, deserves love and affection. Narcissus is enthusiastic about the worship experienced by empathy, and even receives a boost of energy because of his constant insecurity and frustration over everything that changes. They feel confident knowing that empathy will never abandon them, and their ability to sustain empathy as a confident victim easily means that narcissus, if he is knowledgeable, may have energy reserves for life. Remember that if you think of a narcissist, you send him energy. Empathy tends to be easily obsessed because we feel every breeze that changes, every intersection on the vibrating path, and every current that changes, so it's not surprising that the narcissus can tilt us down with the slightest hint of feeling. The contempt and chill often used by narcissus may seem like a deep wound to everyone, but for empathy, it is even deeper, and they return to those first intoxicating days of love bombardment when the narcissus kissed like gifts and hugs as if out of fashion, they can become a desperate concern for empathy. The problem is that these hugs are out of fashion and somehow never go back to fashion, and no amount of Reiki readings or angel cards will change that.

3. Healthy and extreme narcissism

Healthy narcissism

Confidence, charisma, or appreciation for his true talents/attributes without those attributes that lead him to believe that he is superior to others are positive qualities encouraged by most societies. The ability to lead and inspire is equally positive qualities. These features can be described as healthy narcissism. Many confident, extroverted, and successful people have a high level of healthy narcissism and self-improvement, believe in themselves, and appear to be limited by challenges and attention. But these positive aspirations lack the belief that they are "better" than any other person or lack the will to act better. Confidence and confidence are healthy, but overconfidence and trust in your positive attributes make you better than other people, going from healthy narcissism to extremes. Trust and self-esteem do not make healthy narcissists empathic or manipulative. These healthy traits should not be confused with unhealthy or harmful narcissistic habits, as is often the case with many online materials. This is in line with Dr. Malkin's discovery that 1% of people achieve very high results in healthy narcissism and very low in extreme narcissism - people who illuminate the room and inspire others instead of weakening them. They see themselves and others through optimistic pink-colored lenses, and encourage and inspire others instead of feeling threatened by their success.

Extreme narcissism

Narcissistic sacrifice, attention, and superiority .All comments enjoy, to some extent, positive feedback, focus, and approval as a reward for doing good or being in a certain way, but those who highly rate narcissism (both healthy and extreme) delight us more and more. People with extreme narcissism are starting to need it to maintain well-being, protecting themselves so that they do not fall from above, because the alcoholic will avoid sobriety. Some have shaky self-esteem that goes back to the development of addiction. For everyone, love and worship evoke pleasant sensations, releasing dopamine, a brain reward neurotransmitter. For people with low self-esteem and for those who have problems with the regulation of dopamine levels, this experience may be of particular interest. A pleasant rush acts like a "tonic" to calm down the basic pain sensations by negatively feeling yourself. Dopamine is also released when a person discovers that he has the talent and can somehow be successful, or when he finds an activity or attribute that gives him praise or positive attention (for example, being attractive, being right in sports, having academic talent) or achieve goals at work). For most people, this translates into research and development of skills and interests and is a way to develop healthy narcissism. Many confident and friendly people attract attention and meaning, delighting in acting for others: comedians or talk show presenters such as Ellen DeGeneres or James Corden. These people probably don't hide extreme narcissism; they will probably be polite, outgoing, and confident. In people who initially felt abandoned, bad or "low value," positive feelings gained through attention and approval can lead to the habit of continually looking for similar experiences in an unhealthy way, maintaining their ego by ritual pumping it, getting care of being kind, attractive, successful or intelligent. This is called "narcissistic compliment," and the term "supply" is used similarly to addictive drugs. Not only that, but after using or releasing a large amount of dopamine during narcissistic "growth" of supply, some people may be "shocked" in a similar but less extreme way than a drug addict.

Cocaine can peak and then fall when its dopamine levels rise and fall. This can result in a fast mood cycle and a constant search for more supply to maintain standards. Side effects of the sharp decrease in dopamine levels include feelings of depression, anxiety, and irritability. These cycling moods would do nothing for the extreme narcissist's self-esteem, primarily if low self-esteem existed before the addiction. Guilt and shame can exacerbate the cycle, causing extreme narcissus to remain inflated and deny what is close to him when it breaks and how it interacts with the world. Those who score high in extreme narcissism can become competitive because of the limited 'offer' they receive from those around them. If we imagine the attention of an individual as a small packet of "drugs," we can see how it works. The amount of drugs is limited, and the addict wants a lot for himself. Extreme narcissists are often threatened and envious of the people around them, reacting violently to maintain their offer and a sense of "goodness," "correction," or superiority. They can use many forms of manipulation to get as much narcissism as possible, justifying it. The experiences of releasing dopamine, such as drinking alcohol, taking drugs, sex, or smoking, are addictive because of this. The pleasant release of dopamine and the overstated self-esteem of the narcissistic offer escape from naturally low levels of dopamine or the pain of feeling that the narcissus is somehow defective or "bad." At the highest points of the spectrum, the constant need for validation and worship can reach insurmountable levels where no amount of "offer" is sufficient to maintain an inflated sense of narcissus's self-worth. Perceived criticism or mistakes made by a sensitive narcissist can lead to an almost immediate and paralyzing return to this state of low self-esteem. However, when we are in danger, our cognitive protection can be extremely skillful in protecting us from experiencing this kind of pain. Responses to narcissistic defense can intervene to block the threat and "save" the narcissist from facing what it would mean for others to take responsibility for his actions. For those who are lower on a narcissistic scale, this is shown as the most narcissistic part that becomes defensive and does not take responsibility for its offensive words and actions. They can attack in response to any insults or perceived threat to their self-esteem. However, for a person, this choice between taking responsibility and maintaining a defense can make the difference between staying afloat and functionality and being completely broken down.

Can extreme narcissists love?

The claim that narcissists "cannot love" is an overly simplistic and negative view that does not analyze the technical aspects of what is happening between high and narcissistic defense. This idea forgets about the nuances and complications of people. To say that all narcissistic mothers cannot love their children or that a narcissistic spouse cannot love their partner is an unrealistic black and white thought. What's going on People who have features of extreme narcissism often swell to feel good, defend themselves against "shocks" and protect their ego from injury, which means they can think a lot about themselves without too much time thinking about others, If people who show a high frequency of extreme narcissistic tendencies may feel love in the usual sense, it probably depends on the individual. Of course, they can suffer from the same "crushed" response as the rest of us, releasing and "hooking" dopamine and feel that they fall in love. Ironically, falling in love may seem like a pleasant experience with a loved and idolized couple, but it turned out to be selfish. Lovers try to meet their emotional needs, instead of empathy primarily with partners (it has been shown that those who receive unrequited love are more capable of understanding with the "in love" part of the person who is a lover can empathize with them). If the feelings of falling in love from extreme narcissists resemble the experiences of healthier people, then they can be discussed. If these feelings transform into feelings of romantic love, and thus a sense of attachment comparable to more youthful people, they are ambiguous and may vary from person to person. Most lower-level narcissistic people who spend most of their time "without shooting" are perfectly capable of feeling love and empathy in these moments. However, extreme narcissistic people may fear to fall in love because they may consider themselves unworthy or incapable. This can cause fear of the pain and sensitivity that love will bring when their partner abandons or betrays them. However, just because they are afraid of them, deny them, or have little time to sacrifice them, it does not mean that they are insensitive. They may not be able to express it healthily. If the feeling of vulnerability, when they fall in love, causes them anxiety, they can try to alleviate this feeling through infidelity, reduce their partner, creating many attachments to reduce the strength of their original attachment, or try to reduce the value of their love. Somehow partner.

Love and compassion for others cannot be prioritized when narcissistic reactions occur. The opportunity to obtain supplies or the need to defend against the threat to the ego must first decrease before feelings of love appear or express. In cases where these activities are conducted full-time, respect and empathy can never happen. Defending against emotional pain occupies an essential place on the brain's automatic priority list. Love is lower on the list of automatic brain priorities. This does not mean that love is less appreciated by our logical minds or our value systems. This means that the mechanical responses of our brain (which are subconscious and unconscious) move first to protect us from emotional pain before considering higher concepts such as love and empathy. Learn more about real examples of expressing love in narcissistic relationships in Chapter 2.

Extreme narcissists who abuse their lovers

The higher the person is on the scale, the more likely it is that narcissus will see other people as objects for his pleasure. They cannot be considered or loved and can only be there to take what they can. They often pay off only if it helps them get more. Some narcissists are about to idolize their lovers and friends, suddenly seeing their flaws, devaluing them, and rejecting them without thinking. Often they will have a new lover or friend who has been waiting for a change of attention. If this has happened to you, you'll know how devastating and confusing it can be, because the narcissus can move from being the center of your world not to seem to worry about you being there. In some cases, however, they can stop lovers, friends, and family members when needed, chasing them and recovering if they think they are losing interest. Keeping in touch can be helpful because they may need sex or attention later when their supply options are low.

Chapter 7 - Narcissistic scale

Narcissism is not a rare feature. This is a common feature that occurs in people, but only in different amounts. The truth is that almost everyone will have certain features that will introduce us to the scale of narcissism. The concept of spectrum is derived from physics, and the frequency of narcissism indicates the severity of a person's condition. In the range of narcissism, you'll see that narcissists share personal meaning and high ego. However, the degree of sensitivity of a person and his sense of greatness will vary. Psychologists often use this scale of narcissism to test the level of narcissism and diagnose a narcissistic personality disorder. The spectrum of narcissism ranges from 0 to 10. The lower the number, the less narcissistic a person is. The higher the number, the more narcissistic a person is. Those in the middle usually have a balanced amount of narcissism that is healthy. Half of the spectrum includes people who are part of healthy narcissists. They are realistic and have stable features. People with a higher frequency have more harmful elements. They have a sense of arrogance instead of healthy self-esteem. They are more aggressive than assertive and can become surrender. The higher the number, the more self-centered man will be. They will have destructive behavior traits and unhealthy thought processes. Therefore, it should be concluded that it is not good to be too high or too low on this scale. The ideal position in the spectrum is in the middle. Let's take a look at the various numbers on the size and their meaning:

Level 0 in the range is an indicator of an incredibly low amount of narcissism. A person set to 0 is usually too selfless and can be easily manipulated by others. They look after others more than their needs and will easily succumb to others. These people are terrific and humble. However, they lack self-esteem and self-esteem. Level 1 in the spectrum has slightly better people than 0. These people pay a little more attention to their personal needs. However, these people do not trust social gatherings and usually avoid social interaction. They are easily overwhelmed and, therefore, shy. They are also humble, but they have self-esteem. Levels 2 and 3 have more social units. These people can have dreams and goals. They feel more comfortable in social situations than at level 0 or 1. However, these people do not like to be in the spotlight very often. Sometimes they can leave the comfort zone, but they are usually closed. Levels 4, 5, and 6 have people who are on the list of healthy narcissists. These people are humble, but they also have high confidence. They like to attract the attention of others and feel appreciated when it is due. They know when they deserve recognition and when they should let others attract attention. They don't have the unhealthy need to be in the center of everything. They do not fall so low on the spectrum that they avoid care. They have balanced self-esteem and humbleness.

Levels 7 and 8 have slightly more narcissism than they are healthy. They like to show their things and material results. However, they are also inclined to recognize when they are wrong and try to improve. But these people tend to go in and out between good and bad behavior. They like attention and are not wholly stable personalities. Level 9 has people who develop awareness and recognition. They always try to be in the center of things. However, at some point, they realize their unrealistic need for attention and praise. It makes them guilty, but they still try to hide their guilt. They know that paying constant attention to them is terrible, but they seem to be unable to resist. Level 10 is at the end of the spectrum. This includes people who are very selfish and arrogant. Such people have a great idea of themselves and are people classified as NPD. It is known that they are ready to do anything to get what they want. They will lie, cheat, steal, etc., and will do anything to attract attention. They love to show superiority and make others feel inferior. There are three types of unhealthy narcissus. Their personalities are different, but they are all narcissistic in a harmful way. The characteristic feature of these three types of people is that they consider themselves better and better than others. Extrovert narcissists: they are noisy and unpleasant people who love attention. They are very friendly and love to be in social situations. They live to be the center of attention at every meeting. They are those who always publish photos on social networks and love to present their long life and expensive shopping. They will glory until the kingdom arrives when they achieve something. Introvert narcissus: they are afraid of being judged by others, and people can avoid it. They consider themselves better than others, but they don't want others to know. They prefer the company and enjoy the silence in the sense of superiority. Urban skiers: these are people who like to show that they always do it for others without asking for anything in return. They want others to recognize that they are a savior for people and that they always give more than they ever get. Now you can see how different narcissistic people can be. You can observe yourself and the people around you to see where they fall into the specter of narcissism. This will allow you to understand your personality better and help you treat it better.

In most cases, people do not know that they are victims of narcissus. They will mistake what they find in a relationship as a regular part of each pair. Even when violence is extreme, people live by denying that their partner is narcissistic. The main reason for this is the excessive flattery and praise they received during the idealization phase. Narcissus knows how to properly start a relationship and make his patient feel attracted to him so that his first days are romantic. Victims are missing and want to come back at this point with their partners, so they will try to do their best. They don't even know when they are being mistreated because they are so attached to the hope that the relationship will improve. Below are some of the signs that may indicate that you are trapped in a network of narcissus.

Common threats

Most narcissists threaten their victims with things they know they don't want to happen. In response, when the victim is threatened, they tend to humiliate themselves, which gives narcissi more opportunities to control them. If your partner is still threatening to leave, that if it weren't for him, you wouldn't get what you got, you're more likely to have an affair with a narcissist. The reason they use this approach is that it is most effective when it comes to raising fear, doubt, and guilt. Your partner issues threats to show that you don't feel comfortable in a relationship. Because they created risks, you will avoid creating problems because you are afraid that they will work. For example, if they threaten to leave you and say they didn't need you, it will be difficult for you to go because you know they will not beg you to stay.

You don't have a sense of yourself

If you feel at the moment that you have no goals or aspirations, then you have given up. At this point in his life, because of the person he is in a relationship with, he put aside his basic desires and needs and sacrificed his emotional well-being to please the perpetrator. Once in his life, he could be full of life; he was oriented on dreams and goals. But now he feels that he is alive to please and meet the goals and needs of his lover. You've reached the point where your life revolves around them, and you have nothing but a relationship. This means that you sacrificed your right forever and satisfied the perpetrator. A healthy relationship does not mean giving up personal safety, friendship, hobbies, and goals, but it will lead you to use your full potential and happy life. In addition to the victims, later, you will find that you are not able to please your partner and that the victims were in vain.

You have health problems

Most people who have a narcissistic relationship live in denial and do everything to hide the challenges and difficulties they face. They will fight to maintain the right image in society while they suffer intensely. If you're in this position, you're trapped in a network of narcissus. Some people go so far as to have serious health problems that they did not have before becoming involved in a relationship. You can look at yourself and understand that you look older compared to most of your peers, which is known as premature aging. The stress, anxiety, and depression you experience in relationships due to chronic abuse can cancel your immune system. At this point, it means that you are susceptible to various physical and mental illnesses and ailments. Also, if you have terrifying nightmares or can't sleep, it's because you experience trauma through visual flashbacks. People in a healthy relationship do not experience such things.

Self-isolation

One of the ways narcissus will use to make sure you fully control it is to isolate it from people close to you. If they know that your parents or friends can help you understand that you are a victim of violence, then they will try to separate you from them. Some narcissists will use a defamatory campaign against you as if you were a personality disorder. Friends will stop trusting you, and others will intentionally avoid you. In other cases, you isolate yourself from friends because you are ashamed of the abuse you experience. If so, you feel that you are laughing among friends. It is essential to realize that by doing this, you strengthen the perpetrator. However, because of guilt and misunderstanding about mental and emotional violence, people will stalk her until it is her fault. Misunderstandings that people, including family and friends, have may undermine the view that narcissus is as violent as Bergman et al. (2011) found in their analysis of how the narcissus uses his manipulation techniques. Therefore, because you are afraid that nobody understands you, you withdraw from society instead of seeking help and avoiding retaliation or trial. If you find yourself in this situation, it is essential to rethink your position because you are stuck in an unhealthy relationship.

If you blame yourself

For abuse, the actions of narcissists are indeed inhuman, but they are not aware of this and prefer to do it to other people. They usually use so-called reverse psychology. In the idealization phase, relationships will behave best. They are engaged in loving, kind, and gentle activities that aim to win their heart and love. In the later stages, they change and become offensive in every respect. They behave hot and cold, which confuses him of who they are. Instead of realizing that their partners are doing it on purpose, most victims take it because of them. Narcissus is perfect in creating love triangles with which he brings another person who may be a stranger or a former lover in connection to terrorize the victim. In this case, the victim tends to internalize the fear that it will not be enough for them, and leads to competition to obtain the aggressor's acceptance and attention. Also, if you compare yourself to others in a healthier and happier relationship, think about why your partner treats others with respect. Of course, you'll have questions like "why me?" which leads to blaming. The truth is you shouldn't blame yourself. A perpetrator is a wrong person, and the reason you have no doubt is that they have trapped you online.

If you're scared

To achieve greater success or to do what you love narcissists in a relationship that flourishes, denying freedom to victims. In this regard, they ensure that what their lovers do, they must approve or comment on it. If you have a relationship in which you need to ask your partner for permission to do certain things, you have no freedom. If you think that if you do this, it will become a threat to your partner, it's time to leave this relationship. Narcissus will teach you to associate areas of success, talent, interests, and joy with cruel and cruel treatments. So you are conditioned to be afraid of success going beyond what your partners accept because you will be reprimanded or revenge for it. Conditioning led to his lack of confidence, anxiety, depression, and, above all, concealing his abilities. It is essential to know that the reason why the perpetrator is limited to doing what you like to achieve greater success is that he knows that if you succeed, they will lose control over you.

If you feel dissociation

You are trapped in a narcissistic network if you feel physically and mentally separated from a sense of identity, awareness, perceptions, and memory. Experts considered dissociation as the essence of trauma. A person in this situation has physical feelings, thoughts, images, sounds, and emotions divided and divided in such a way as to lead their own lives. If you feel emotional numbness even after a terrible event, this is not normal. If repression, addiction, obsessions, and cripples have become your lifestyle because they help you avoid abuse, your partner is a narcissist. This is not normal, but your brain has developed ways to block the effects of pain emotionally so that you don't have to face frightening circumstances. If this happens, you will disconnect yourself from your loved ones, the perpetrator, the environment, and your real personality. At this point, you need to find a trauma-oriented therapist. They will help you assess the situation you are in after joining the items.

You can't expect peace when you meet a real narcissist, someone who has a narcissistic personality disorder. You will experience visceral experience because you will feel a mixture of disgust, helplessness, surprise, anger, and, depending on what is happening, whether it is disappointment or shame. You will explore these emotions deeply. There are many people with whom you will discover that a narcissistic person has hit you. Some people hate this person and will start to hate this emotion. Unfortunately, feelings will still occur. This friend will be the most helpful and friendliest person I have ever met, but his narcissism cuts caution and kindness like a knife. So what should you do when you meet someone who has no empathy, always needs admiration, is arrogant, fantastic, blames you for everything, and dares to brag about himself always? How do you take care of yourself when you meet someone like that? One of the best ways to meet someone when you experience such strong emotions is to face the situation and discuss it with the person who bothers you. This is the best way to deal with the job, but narcissus will never worry about how you feel. Most discussions with daffodils do not help in their disgust, helplessness, or anger. The worst thing is that they argue with the narcissist that it will bring the opposite effect. There was a time when I had to face a narcissist, and this person was the person he cared about. I spent hours writing the script and thinking carefully. I shared with them what I felt, and I was also aware of how that person felt and what could pass through his mind. All I got was anger and guilt. The reaction surprised me because I was trying to face this person and let him know how I felt. So how do you talk and react to narcissus? Let's take a look at the following tips:

Always look at the bigger picture

You must remember to look at the larger picture. You cannot expect change or control over another person, but you can change the way that person controls or influences you. You should always ask yourself what is most important in every situation. Narcissus knows how to capture you and completely devour you. Their stories and insights will still absorb you, and you must realize this as quickly as possible and look at the big picture. This person is only one of the 8 billion people on this planet. So why would you let someone have such power over your emotions?

Always look at your strengths

First, you need to try to identify those qualities that are more energetic in you. Therefore, you should use these features as strengths. Sit still and write down your five forces. When interacting with the narcissus, observe these features and remain calm. You should ensure that you always use your strengths to stay healthy.

Avoid toxicity

It is difficult to face someone who makes it difficult for them to lead a good life. Therefore, you can altogether avoid the situation, which leads to many other problems. For example, if you prevent a condition that causes anxiety, anxiety can get worse. In the event of toxicity, avoid exposure to fumes as the fumes can cause kneeling. You should always consider your character as your strength. It will help you regulate emotions, so it will be easier to control your impulses when you are close to a narcissist. You should always use your strengths to spend time on non-toxic effects.

Use a narcissist

You should always ask yourself what features or behavior does the narcissus express or harm. You need to spend some time and try to understand what bothers you. Is it because they underestimate their goodness or honesty? Do you pretend to be spiritual? Are they human? Most likely, forces that you minimize or overestimate are of great importance to you. These strengths are called shortcut buttons. If someone does not show you these strengths, he perceives them as insane. Your knowledge of yourself will increase when you find out what switches are essential to you. So you can use this knowledge to your advantage when dealing with conflicts or problems.

Always be very sensitive to the behavior of others. When dealing with someone who is narcissistic but has no narcissistic personality disorder, it's a good idea to understand the person's behavior. You should take the time and try to understand the strengths of the person, as well as assess the advantages that he used in excess or insufficiently. This will help in maintaining the goal to see the characteristics of the person. If a person has a narcissistic personality disorder, he will exhibit unhealthy behavior that affects his cognition. For these people, it is difficult to identify the strengths that are abused or underused. If one does not feel compassion for others, one cannot perceive him as not using social intelligence or kindness.

Similarly, one cannot see a quick temperament and the need to admire it as potential underuse. This kind of behavior requires an entirely different interpretation. This is because these people misuse their strengths. He will need to understand if the narcissus uses his character's resistance to hurt or manipulate others intentionally. Research shows that people often use perseverance and creativity for harmful purposes. These people can also use other character powers to strengthen and overthrow another person. You must choose one of the strategies listed in this chapter and start taking care of yourself. Narcissus won't worry about it, but you can do it.

Sometimes it is easy to tell if someone is narcissistic, and in some cases, this is not possible. The manifestation of narcissism can vary from person to person. As we have already noted, there are six types of narcissus, and each category is different from each other. Exhibitionists, junkies, stalkers, and psychopaths are easily recognized. These three types of narcissi openly show their narcissistic behavior. They are not afraid to declare their feelings and do not refuse to act. Persecuting narcissists can be confused with ordinary criminals.

On the other hand, hidden narcissists and seducer could never be recognized. They are much hidden and implement their plans in a calculating way. One of the critical factors that help to identify narcissists is that their intentions are similar. Although some may seem friendly, the ultimate goal of the narcissist is domination.

All narcissists think they are better and will use all means possible to gain dominance. Even those who use seduction show the first signs of their final intentions. From the very beginning, the narcissus will try to take control of his thoughts and mind. Narcissus is aimed at people whom he wants to control and those he considers most vulnerable. Narcissism manifests itself in two main ways: emotional reaction and sober behavior. Emotional response refers to the way a person reacts when they are in a particular emotional state. Narcissistic behavior is easily manifested when someone is angry or sad. When narcissistic people get nervous, they react abusively, be it verbally, emotionally, sexually, or physically.

Actions that someone performs when they are angry or sad play an essential role in determining their personality. Sober response refers to the actions and decisions that a person makes when he is sober. Studying someone's daily activities, words, and activities can help determine narcissism. Narcissistic people generally show anger and anger, even if they have not been offended. In everyday activities, narcissists are perfectionists. They usually relate daily activities to successful people they admire. Their words are full of praise for themselves and quickly make friends with people who praise them while rejecting those who criticize them. Recognizing a narcissistic person is not accessible if you do not pay attention to what surrounds you. The ability to acknowledge narcissism begins with self-awareness. Before you realize the narcissist's actions and emotions, you must be able to recognize your feelings. The ability to understand and manage emotions and the emotions of others is known as the emotional intelligence EQ. In psychology, we are talking about people who can study and manage other people's feelings, people with high EQ. People with high EQ are not easy to manipulate. Narcissi exploit people who do not have emotional intelligence. People with low EQ are easy to manage. Their ideological principles can influence them, and you can often find followers of others. We will go further into the concept of emotional intelligence and its impact on personal relationships. With this in mind, if you're interested and pay attention to everything around you, it's easy to detect narcissism. You can recognize narcissism by observing someone's daily activities, paying attention to their visions and dreams, observing their perception of others, observing their reaction to emotional problems, among others. Five ways to recognize a narcissus

Narcissists are very responsive to criticism and opposition

As mentioned earlier, narcissists are susceptible to people. They react explosively to problems that others would not do. If you realize that someone does not accept criticism, corrections, or anything that looks negative, you should start to look closely at their actions. The fact is that few people appreciate negative comments. However, although most people do not like negative feedback, the narcissist's reaction is explosive in addition to resistance. Narcissists consider themselves excellent and do not accept comments or suggestions that might indicate otherwise. If you ask a narcissist who can reveal his weaknesses, he rushes to lie to protect himself from showing weaknesses. This behavior of narcissistic individuals has been described as a narcissistic dilemma. This is because narcissists often have the dilemma of whether to show their real personality and accept their weaknesses or to use a false character and never accept their shortcomings. It is believed that the main reason why most narcissists are so defensive is because of fears and weaknesses that they do not want other people to see. Narcissists have low self-esteem for what they want to create the world.

Show low self-esteem

If you're not emotionally intelligent, you'll never be able to read low self-esteem among narcissists. They try to cover their self-esteem with an overly glorified personality. Narcissists boast of all areas of life in which they are the weakest. You will find a person who lacks the wealth and is associated with the wealthiest people in the world. According to them, they are ashamed to be reduced. They do not want to be associated with poverty and therefore cover it, assuming they have money. They will combine everything they possess with wealth and class. They intend to buy only high-end products and do not believe that anyone else can have a more valuable item than theirs. All these factors act on the sign of low self-esteem. In relationships, they can become aggressive and accuse the other partner of cheating without evidence. Most narcissistic partners become aggressive only because of paranoia, not because they have been deceived. If a narcissistic person thinks that he is not worthy of having someone as a life partner, he threatens and tries to instill fear in him. The narcissist is afraid of being left alone. Narcissi use anxiety, bullying, and bullying to hide their low self-esteem. Even if they never agree that they have low self-esteem, they can trust a friend or someone too close. Most narcissi have an inner personality that they try to hide. Some narcissists develop a narcissistic personality because of childhood traumatic events. They stay in the child's mentality for a long time and defend their character against exposure. They are usually afraid to face their childhood fears and give up something that would stop them. To detect weakness and low self-esteem in a narcissistic person, you need to be very careful. You must pay attention to each word spoken and its measures. From time to time, they will give terms of penance and repentance.

Narcissists are too honest and defensive

Narcissists have an infinite need to defend their actions. They are people who do things that can be described as unfortunate and still find a way to protect them. Narcissists are not criticized for this treason. They are pretentious, exaggerated, stubborn, and self-defense. Every word that comes out of their mouth is directed at self-defense. Even if they are part of a group, they tend to distinguish themselves from group errors; but they are in a hurry to celebrate the group's success. Narcissi don't like working in a group because they believe that group members may not meet the standards set in their minds. When they work in a team, they control and eventually lead to differences in the group. Narcissi are friendly only with people who follow their paths or with those who are afraid of them. They do not make friends with people who question their way of thinking. They must be right, even if the facts do not add up.

Interestingly, they attach too much importance to everything they do to make sure that it was done correctly. When they fail, they express anger and anger at everyone. In the workplace, they quickly blame other employees for their mistakes. In his words, there is no known vocabulary for an apology. They will never use the word "sorry," even if it is clear that they have made a mistake.

He is easily nervous

The reaction of narcissists to words, opinions, and actions of other people is the most obvious sign of narcissism. Narcissi are known to be very sensitive people because of their delicate personality. They are angry because of problems that others cannot call anyone. His anger is mainly due to words or deeds that appear to contradict his ideologies. However, this type of reaction also occurs in people with other personality disorders. For example, Boarder personalities and very sensitive people show anger when questioned. For narcissi, their passion stems from the fact that challenges can show them as weak or that they can prevent them from achieving their goal. In this case, most narcissists try to hide their weaknesses, dominating. For example, if a narcissistic person is interested in a sexual partner, it's easy to say his narcissistic personality by rejecting his terms. Even seductive narcissists are still victims of anger. The best way to recognize seductive narcissists is to frustrate their efforts continually. Seductive narcissists are usually patient to some extent; with time, however, they become impatient and begin to show anger. Any action that makes him appear weak or unworthy will irritate. Angry narcissists are physically or emotionally aggressive. They'll start with threats and then become aggressive.

Narcissists design traits, traits, and personalities that they do not take into account

In most cases, narcissists exhibit features that are not part of their material. Because they believe that if they keep saying they are good or love, they will hide their real personality from the public. Most narcissi never accept their real character. They will work with charismatic leaders and other successful people. His true identity remains inside. If you're interested, you'll quickly notice that they say they are something they are not. In short, the characters they choose help them to devalue and slander others. They will focus on the flaws of others and report bugs so that no one can focus on them. They believe that if they highlight the weaknesses of other people, they stand out as the right ones. Narcissists quickly evaluate and always find a way to get something terrible from everyone around them. In this way, they focus all negative energies on other people, trying to protect their personality.

Understanding the personality of narcissus is not accessible if you are not interested. They hide their real identity very well. Sometimes they can use manipulation, and in some cases, they use force. Catching in any situation is not good. Most narcissi begin with mental manipulations. If they find that they can easily fall into their charm, they will hide the remaining symptoms. However, if he is emotionally intelligent than they think, they resort to physical violence. You must be careful to protect yourself from all forms of narcissistic bullying. If you allow prolonged narcissistic use, you'll eventually be brainwashed and lose the ability to make the right decisions. Victims of narcissistic abuse need years to regain health, and some never recover. It is your responsibility to protect yourself from such people by being observers. Read the signs early enough and separate yourself from your line of thought.

The secret language of narcissus, psychopaths, and sociopaths.

Understanding their language is the only way to protect yourself from narcissi. According to statistics, 1 in 25 people in UU in the United States. You have symptoms of narcissism, psychopaths, or sociopaths. The secret language of narcissists, sociopaths, and psychopaths is the same. We will examine each of these ailments as we go deeper. One of the external features of narcissus is selfishness. They share this character with sociopaths and psychopaths. According to Dr. Martha Stout at Harvard Medical School, people who exhibit NPD speak the language of madness, the words salad, pathological jealousy, and gaslighting. The style of the narcissistic person follows the cycle of narcissism, which we will see later. It is necessary to study and understand the narcissistic cycle to detect its charm. Initially, some narcissists are fascinating and attractive. You may not be able to tell a narcissist when you know him because he is wearing a mask. At first, they can be cute, fun and very romantic. They can push for what is right for you and even lead you to success in one field or another. Some narcissistic people seem so harmless and are wrapped up when they develop a friendship. They will win your trust and make you believe that you have your best interests in mind. In the first phase of the cycle, anyone can fall into the trap. However, some tips should give you a signal. If you realize that a person is using your success to glorify yourself, step back. Narcissi can force him to succeed so that they can be seen as winners.

In some cases, they even donate to charity to show themselves as loving people. Narcissists always have a hidden personal motive in their actions. If you realize that a person relates to your success as your success, be careful. Such people are too possessive too. Although someone may call you "my or my" narcissist, he is also possessed to show off and refer to you possessively. The language of sociopaths and psychopaths consists of chronic manipulation. Like narcissists, psychopaths, and sociopaths, they must first capture their victims. They will attract a person to their network using brainwashing and manipulation techniques. Some use their abuses to brainwash and evaluate the individual. Narcissi and sociopaths use emotional abuse to devalue the individual. They ensure that the victim feels useless and is ready to follow his instructions without asking questions. Victims of daffodils generally fall into anxiety, fear, and futility, and in some cases, experience suicidal thoughts.

In most cases, a narcissistic person seeks to transform the victim into an object. They turn to anyone they point to a puppet that they can check for complacency. The main reason narcissistic use is hazardous is that the authors point to emotional strength. In human psychology, the cerebral circuit of physical and emotional pain is the same. In other words, if it causes physical pain, such as a blow to the face or uses offensive terms, it has the same effect on the brain. A person who experiences verbal violence every day may suffer many emotional injuries and may have difficulty regaining health for a long time. Emotional scars are difficult to remove, and most narcissistic victims have extreme PTSD or PTSD.

Learning a psychopathic and sociopathic narcissistic language helps protect against its patterns. An essential factor that you must understand is that cruelty among narcissists is not explicit but implied. His actions and his desire to hurt are so deeply rooted in his works. Everything they do, from facial expressions to gestures, sounds, and words, often doesn't suit their actions. His cruelty is purposeful, and his actions do not cause remorse. In most cases, terms of penance and repentance are part of the language by which the victim is online. In narcissist's language, verbal tools are many. All communication tools have been designed to cause pain and peace when needed. They are intended to weaken the victim's self-esteem and increase the narcissus. In their arsenal, they will use cruel tools such as sarcasm, insults, change of guilt, sadistic imitation, silence, etc. Narcissistic individuals are friendly when their presence makes them see the world better. Any attempt to undermine your comfort reveals negativity in your personality. Here are some tips to help you understand the language used by psychopaths, sociopaths, and narcissists:

No empathy

If you find that you are working or dating someone who has no empathy, you should start trading carefully. At first, they can be caring and accommodating. However, the key is how they treat other people. Check if the person shows the same empathy towards family members such as their brothers or sisters, mother or father. The way a person treats other family members will show their real personality. Most narcissists will never introduce their partner to family or friends. If you're in a relationship with someone who can't add you to friends or family, start reading the red flags. The closeness of family members will emphasize the real character of the person. An evil man can easily pretend to be with you, but he will quickly explode in front of his brother. Most narcissistic people don't have a good relationship with other family members.

Watch out for selfishness

Egoism is a language that dominates the life of narcissists. In the early stages, they can pretend to give you everything you want. The best way to find out if they are selfless or just setting a trap, watch them act on other people. His actions towards other people represent his real personality. When a person is in love or obsessed with someone, he can offer favorable treatment. However, treatment slowly subsides, and the real character of the person creeps in.

Secret characters

Narcissistic individuals are compassionate and restrained. The first clue to understanding a language is to look for your real personality. When you try to ask personal questions and look for evidence, narcissistic people quickly become defensive—Narcissi bloom on lies. Press to learn the truth about your past, previous relationships, family life, etc. Such questions should be asked early before the narcissus takes complete control over his mind.

Why are we attracting daffodils?

Victims of narcissistic abuse often have PTSD or narcissistic abuse syndrome. For many doctors, it is still a great secret how far the effects of narcissistic bullying can reach. However, the obvious factor is that victims always blame themselves. A person who becomes a victim of narcissistic abuse is not guilty. In most cases, the people who fall victim are innocent and easily trust the people they interact with. Victims generally do not see evil in people, but rather trust the good intentions of all. Fallen people, victims of narcissists, are people who have adopted a life of freedom and impose no restrictions. They are carefree and do not care too much about what the world has to say. They are people ready to enjoy life and have fun. They accept the risk and are prepared to give a chance of love, even if the changes do not add up.

Nobody attracts narcissists. It is the narcissist who sees the person and idealizes him as a victim. Just because a narcissus is attacking you doesn't mean you are weak in any way. It is the narcissist who considers the person a cousin. Narcissi seek weak and defenseless victims. However, narcissistic individuals can manipulate any occasion. The strategy they adopt can leave everyone behind. The first step for a narcissist is to remove the target victim from friends and family. They manipulate their victims to make sure that they have no one in their lives who could ask for help. When they have a victim there, they start to hurt. There are three main reasons why a narcissist can be attracted to a particular person.

For self-worship

Narcissists like to show their superiority over others. They want to show that they are better and deserve the best things in life. When a narcissist sees a person who can help achieve this state, he is attracted to it. You can have a friend who is only your friend because it increases your social status. Narcissi are looking for people who will raise them to a higher level. Unfortunately, when they make friends with the person they desire, they try to maintain this relationship through abuse. Narcissists will be attracted by the most beautiful girl or the most attractive man. They will lure the victim into the trap by seducing them. When a person enters their claws, they will try to close them, using abuse, intimidation, and threats. Narcissists cannot maintain relationships because their real personality is hidden. The initial complaint is eventually eliminated and replaced by manipulation to maintain the relationship. The narcissist's ultimate goal is to ensure that the manipulator does not escape. Their goal is to continue to benefit from having a sacrifice in their lives. If they don't maintain this relationship with reasonable social standards, they resort to abuse.

Narcissi attract people who are perceived as weak

If a narcissist considers him a weak person, he may try to use him to achieve some ambitions. Narcissists attack vulnerable people to inflict pain on complacency. They also appeal to vulnerable people as personal worshipers. Narcissists want people to praise them and talk about them well in public.

They will point to someone who can manipulate and become a puppet for self-worship.

Narcissistic target persons for material benefits

Narcissists can tell anyone who thinks they have something they want. They can affect a person through manipulation or intimidation. They will try to get money or property from someone without using force, but eventually, they can become aggressive. Narcissi don't care if you're still poor or not. They will financially exhaust someone to the last penny and then reject the victim. In many cases, such people use love to lure victims into a trap. They are looking for people who can desperately desire love and focus on them.

Narcissus are attracted to very talented people

Narcissists are often obsessed with fame, money, and titles. They can point to someone who enjoys such high positions to develop their intentions. They want someone they can work with to increase their status. In some cases, the goal may be material gain or complacency. Narcissus will have sex with a known person to show that he is worth a higher social status.

There, we learn to look at ourselves and the world, where we accumulate good habits such as cleaning and industry; and where we adopt corrupt practices, and sometimes, depending on our development, much worse. Some mental disorders are a direct result of our education. Things like a sociopath, borderline personality disorder, and narcissistic personality disorder have their source in child abuse and neglect and have lasting consequences in adulthood. Sometimes these problems are detected in advance by especially aware parents or teachers; other times nobody notices it because nobody knows what to look for. In this chapter, we discuss narcissism in families, examining both narcissistic parents and narcissistic children and siblings.

Meet Margarita

Daisy is a charming thirty-four-year-old woman with a good job, pleasant department, and active social life. She's lost weight since college, but she still doesn't do much exercise, and this shows, but it's not enough for someone who calls her "fat." She also lives in the same city as the recently widowed mother and sees her on weekends to help with household chores and housework in her childhood home. As Daisy approaches, she sees the sports trophies won by older sister Ellen, who is now married and lives across the country. The entire library is dedicated to the memories of Ellen, a competition for children that Ellen won during sports days at the university.

Mom was a sports trainer and loved to enjoy her team's victories, speak at the awards ceremony, and even interview the local newspaper. So he financed all these activities for Ellen and saw his daughter's results as his own. Ellen loved to focus her mother's attention and, over time, began to do things to make sure he would keep her. He began to bully Daisy subtly and openly. He would comment on Daisy's hair or clothes or call her "ugly," "stupid," or "fat," even if Daisy wasn't that kind. He broke Daisy's toys and intentionally turned his head away from his Barbie dolls to prevent Daisy from playing with them. When Daisy complained about her sister, her mother did not believe her. Instead, he complained that Daisy was no longer like Ellen. That was the problem with Daisy's mother that Daisy wasn't like Ellen. During her development, Daisy was not interested in competitions, nor was she particularly interested in sports, preferring martial arts and photography. I wanted to study Aikido and learn to take astronomical photos, but my mother was not involved in photography and thought that martial arts would make Daisy "too violent." So, not seeing any of them, he refused to support Daisy but offered to pay if he wanted to become an intermediary like his sister.

Because her dreams die of the plant and her father defends her mother's decision, Daisy pointed out two things that her mother did not control: school and food. Outstanding in high school, joining all the academic clubs and activities that she could to keep her as far away from home as possible and altogether avoid sport. She was gaining weight, to her mother's horror and her sister's entertainment. He then enrolled in a good state university, founded the traditional "Freshman 10" and earned another thirty pounds before graduation. He also worked hard at his lectures, compiling the director's list and graduating from Summa Cum Laude with a degree in finance. While her academic degrees and awards have received praise from her father, Daisy's mother and sister responded well enough to look good at the people around her, but they never showed interest or pride that Ellen had succeeded. And retransmit Regarding Daisy's weight, her mother called her "fat" and "Pudge-Pot," while supporting Ellen's athletic figure as a reference standard. Her sister just teased her and called her "fat." When she was an adult, Daisy almost completely abandoned her mother and sister's life. They met for the first time in memory of their father a few days after his death. Ellen, now a mother and a successful fitness instructor, was kind to her sister, but Daisy recognized the smiles and stains under her face. The mother looked at her and said that she was happy that Daisy finally appeared, although later in the evening, she heard her mother and sister comment on her weight. After the death of her father, Daisy began to feel the pressure to do little things for her mother. This did not involve excuses or requests for a better relationship but consisted of the firm insistence of mother and sister that Daisy was responsible for her. "You can at least look after her," said Ellen. The cousins he had an eye on called his mother, and he wanted to know why he would not spend time with his mother, never accepting that Daisy's childhood was beautiful, like her sister. "She's alone now," they said. "It was a long time ago, and I'm sure it wasn't too bad." It was a routine, and Daisy finally gave up, but soon regretted that she did. When he goes to visit his mother, he comes to the following variant: the mother brags about Ellen, talks about how beautiful she is, how carefree, where she goes with her husband this summer, or during the holidays. How smart she is, what a great job she did at the competition, and how wonderful it is that her daughter, Taylor, follows her footsteps, starting with the game and athletics. This influences critical comments about Daisy's weight and figure, her work, and how to find better someone to support her because, as Mom is happy to point out, "you're sure you can't take care of yourself." This topic became so constant that he slips into phone calls and sometimes even in emails, which made Daisy feel like she was a child: angry, exhausted, and depressed.

Narcissistic parents

The story of Daisy is the story of an adult son of an evil narcissist. In her most basic form, her mother saw her children as a reflection of herself, not as separate people. As a result, the daughter who made her mother look beautiful in the most obvious way, thanks to the achievements on the racetrack and the racetrack, who married a rich man and is now a jet, receives all praise, increasing yours. Daughter in the same way as she was raised; while the single Marguerite, who has no children to brag about and whose life was one of the academic achievements that his mother was unable to understand or failed to understand, led a quiet academic life, is pushed into a close relationship with his mother she raped her mother and her team of "flying monkeys," cousins and sister, and then they were subjected to the same criticism and mockery as before. In the eyes of her mother, Daisy does not represent her in the way she thinks her daughter represents her, and she is too academic and too fat. For Daisy's mother, a woman of athletic shape, with strong muscles instead of soft curves, is the personification of female beauty and the peak of desire. Here is how he sees himself what Ellen has become, and this is how it should be.

On the other hand, she sees Daisy's smooth and tortuous body as fat, weak, and undesirable. All this means that Daisy will be a frequent target of the mother's narcissistic anger. If we share it, we will see that children like Daisy tend to feel: completely devalued, deeply afraid of defending hypersensitivity to the feelings of others, unable to protect against the emotions of others, chronically uncertain, so they always ask themselves questions. Concerned about how others perceive them as deeply insecure about relationships, generally considering them unsatisfactory or even toxic. Deeply cynical, seeing narcissism in all people with whom they have contact. Used and spent at work or school, having no idea why everything and everyone makes them live in such a difficult time.

Daisy's story shows the strength of these feelings, especially her sense of devaluation and uncertainty about relationships, but also illustrates the great importance of external validation for a narcissist, as well as her exaggerated sense of law. Your self-esteem and armor depend on it to protect your inner weakness and sensitivity. In this case, my mother was an athlete and the coach of the winning high school team. She experienced external confirmation that her team's victories gave her life, the status she gave her as a coach, and she felt desperately empowered to get her daughters back, transforming them into her perfect reflexes.

How can a mother do this?

For people with a narcissistic personality disorder, it's less about 'how' and more about 'why.' The "how" part is simple: they can't resist. As to why they do this, this is because their nature as evil narcissists leaves them without emotional empathy and with a sense of full right, especially those who consider themselves inferior. Finally, narcissus will show a distorted view of others and the world around them, which therapists call "uniqueness," the assumption that everyone thinks in the same way as narcissus, and especially his notions of good and evil. They are unable to look at the situation outside their point of view, which they consider the only right picture. Because they do not understand that there may be other, but equally important ways of seeing something, they react with hostility as if they were personally criticized and insulted.

This treatment affected Daisy and Ellen in several ways

Daughters' nature is to seek love and approval from their mother, and Daisy and Ellen are no different. However, in her case, constant judgment and intimidation resulted in sending two young women to different paths. Ellen internalized her mother's standards and values and became the reflection that the mother was looking for, and even raised her daughter in the image of her mother. As for Ellen, he went the other way, rebelling against his mother's tyranny, while paying the price. After all, when it came to her mother, Daisy was still part of her and owed her obedience. From Daisy's point of view, her mother's requests were impossible to fulfill unless they were what she was and even wanted to be. Now, as an adult subject to the same behavior, Daisy has a choice, and the more her mother tries to intimidate her, the easier this choice will be.

Raise narcissistic children

Narcissism is a feature that comes from the way someone asks, and the question is: what parenting practices lead to narcissism in children? He is divided into an emphasis on self-esteem and direct happiness of the child, as opposed to his self-sufficiency, limitations, and discipline.

Everyone gets a trophy

No. They do not have. This is the answer for people from previous generations. Although this may be shocking to the current crop of young parents, there was a time when there were definitive winners and losers and when it was necessary to win prizes. It was a paradigm that reflected how the world really works. Unfortunately, some people think they are doing their children a favor by focusing on their happiness and self-esteem, excluding discipline and positive and constructive feedback. They think they are doing their children a favor by making sure they receive a prize regardless of their efforts. This paralyzes their ability to become self-sufficient adults and reinforces the belief that they are the center of the universe and that they deserve praise and reward regardless of their achievements or shortcomings, which are the first steps to educate a narcissist.

Social networks and narcissism

If there is one thing that children and young adults have not had in previous generations, this is a ubiquitous social network. Once private moments, thoughts are written in the newspaper, photos in the album; now, they flow forever in cyberspace on platforms such as Facebook, Twitter, and Instagram, open to the view, comments, and judgment of the world. For many, I like them, forward them, share them, affect self-esteem, and for many others, these things feed their narcissism. What's more, it allowed them to take their narcissism to new and harmful levels. After all, in the past very few people were interested in what you did at dinner, during your last trip to the mall, the selfie you did at the fair or in the bathroom, showing the new Daffy Duck tattoo you did in your finish, With the development of social networks everything, even the most mundane, risky, grotesque or offensive, is presented to everyone as if people wanted to see many of these things. Some certainly do, especially if the poster is a celebrity, but for the most part, these publications do not make sense to anyone other than an advertisement. However, they are published. Why? Because these publications and their reactions feed poster narcissism. People will post bold photos of themselves or videos of their spitting in an ice cream tub or hitting someone to show their amazement and let people know what they can do and that the things they do are worth it. Behavior. After all, social networking culture teaches people that their feelings, thoughts, opinions, and actions are more relevant to others than they are. It generates a false sense of meaning and significance, increasing the narcissism of a society flooded with selfies and emoticons. Children raised in this environment are more prone to narcissism, especially if their parents or guardians cross the border between raising a child with high self-esteem and raising a narcissist.

Personality development and narcissism

Parents' willingness to develop their children's self-esteem is easily understood, but according to psychologists Eddie Brummelman, Sander Thomas, and Constantine Sedikides, as parents increase their children's self-esteem, they can easily lead to narcissism. Psychologists have been discussing personality formation for some time. Is it genetic, and therefore stable from birth, or is it the result of fluid experience, and accordingly varies depending on the circumstances? The third option is that it begins as a fluid in childhood and solidifies in early adulthood. In this third option, the role of guardians and learned behaviors is the key to developing healthy self-esteem or narcissism. According to Brummelman and his colleagues, there is a significant difference between self-esteem and narcissism. Yes, they both rely on people who perceive how others judge them, but this is where the similarities end and differences have a significant impact on how everyone perceives their social world, themselves, and others. For narcissists, this social world is arranged in vertical hierarchical order, with those above and below. Narcissists do not recognize equals, but only the need to reach the summit with all the means necessary to strengthen their weak self-image with the help of ornaments of supremacy. Each relationship is seen as an opportunity, something that can be used to serve the ultimate goal.

On the other hand, people with high self-esteem see a parallel social world in which everyone is at the same level. They focus on relationships rather than competition and usually see these relationships as goals in themselves. There is a difference between the perception of themselves as higher (narcissism) and the perception of themselves as dignified (high self-esteem).

Narcissus - a bully

When a child moves towards narcissism, we often observe the development of intimidating behavior. After all, persecutors have many features related to narcissus, including an atmosphere of superiority and a sense of law, which hide the weak and often terrified inner self. They are experts in removing guilt and generally manage to avoid the abuse they cause. Even worse, when a child complains to an adult, the teacher says about the stalker, he is often not considered, because by playing the victim, the stalker usually manages to get rid of adults who are trying to deal with the situation. This initiates a cycle of repetitive abuse and unnecessary interventions that will soon undermine the victims' self-esteem.

Character traits indicating the potential for overbearing

 Parents, teachers, and other health care professionals, leaders, and trainers must identify personality traits that lead to bullying. You'll notice that they are all narcissistic features that only strengthen the relationship between bullying and narcissism—the Eddie Haskell effect. Stalkers work hard to make a positive impression on authorities such as parents and teachers. However, if an adult observes for some time, he will notice that the same kindness does not apply to other children when adults do not watch. This is the kind of manipulation that adults should see.

Know everything. This child always thinks he is right, regardless of any evidence to the contrary. This kind of thinking results from the child's need to defend himself against error or sensitivity. This is a sign of deep uncertainty. Bluff. The child wants to tell others how wonderful they are by refusing to listen to the good news of others or assigning them their ideas or results. Baby Pouty If an older child usually kisses when he can't succeed, this is a bad sign. We are not talking about something that the child finds overwhelming, but about the opposite reaction to disappointment. Innocent Because of a lack of guilt or remorse for something they did, the child protests against his innocence, blaming another person, maintaining that position as long as possible, sometimes infinitely long. King of Tyrants. Like Baby Pouty, King Tyrant's attacks during the day are inverse reactions to disappointment, which means not only deep uncertainty but a sense of valid law. Wrong sperm this is a child with an apparent lack of empathy who feels entitled to say or do cruel things with other children. They often do not understand how and why what they say or do is harmful and usually do not care. This is an issue that needs to be resolved quickly. These personality traits indicate intimidating behavior and are closely related to narcissistic personality disorder. Parents, teachers, and other health care professionals must understand and recognize these signs to mitigate any potential harm to the child or other people.

Don't raise a narcissist

Based on their research, Brummel man and his colleagues have determined that it is possible to prevent child narcissism while promoting self-esteem. According to them: parents and teachers should praise children for their results without comparing them with peers. For example, you can say, "Great job!" which conveys courage and effects instead of "You are the best!" who conveys superiority. Parents should encourage children to think about everything they have in common with peers and discourage them from being better than them. Finally, when a child suffers from low self-esteem, adults must do two things in their lives: first, they need to reassure the child of his value, helping him receive positive comments about the fact that people with low self-esteem tend to be indifferent. Secondly, it helps the child correctly process everything that others say about him, helping him understand criticism as constructive comments. Remember that all children deserve a safe and functional childhood. By assisting children in getting out of this kind of deep uncertainty that leads to both narcissism and intimidation, with a lack of empathy and associated responsibility, we help ensure safety and functionality.

Dealing with narcissistic brothers

For narcissistic parents, it is almost inevitable that even one or more children are narcissistic. Children capture parents' behavior and initially learn to cope with the world around them by modeling this behavior and incorporating essential traits in their personality. The father has no empathy in vain, he feels good, and so on teaches his children that "normal" people behave, and then the child internalizes them. This is reinforced by a second parent who generally assumes the role of activator or "flying monkey," who often perpetuates dynamics, shielding narcissus, apologizing, and defending his behavior, continuing even after the death of a narcissistic father. Of course, not all narcissist children become narcissists. Some rebel against the narcissistic father, generally becoming a scapegoat in the family, while the narcissistic child seems to be the favorite, gaining the little love and attention that the narcissistic father could offer and take advantage of the protection provided from the inner flying monkey.

Yes they are trying to catch you

If you think your brother is hurting you intentionally and for no apparent reason, you are not paranoid. They're trying to catch you. One of the hallmarks of a narcissistic brother is that they do everything possible to hurt you. It has nothing to do with what he did or said, but with a lack of parental love. They consider this a limited resource, and you are the competition. They will do everything they can to make sure they understand you, and you don't. This form of bullying is designed to undermine their position in the family, make them feel like strangers without a place that does not deserve the love, attention or support they do, and bullying often goes unnoticed by a narcissistic father, or is ignored, apologized, redirected, and even encouraged because it's convenient. It is challenging to be a narcissist's brother or sister, especially when you realize that they are not growing up and that parents will never help because of the risk of assessing their behavior or responsibility for the situation. In this way, it goes into adulthood, where intimidation tactics that were once aggressive become more subtle, sophisticated, and useful. After all, they are not going to share a legacy with you. Here are some things you can expect from your narcissistic brother: they will betray you in almost every possible way. They will use you in practically every possible way. You will be lied to by commission, omission, obfuscation, and inaccurate details. They will hide important information about the family. They will judge you in an extreme and often hypocritical way. Being close to your family will be extremely hostile towards you, but not towards others. They will show total contempt for important events and milestones in their lives. They will argue with you, assuming you don't know what you're talking about until you want to talk about something meaningful with them.

Nothing changes in adulthood

You may think that when you grow up, everything will change. After all, you and your brother are adults, with adult responsibilities, so is it not time to give up all the behaviors of children? If you were dealing with someone healthy, someone like you, the answer would probably be yes. However, you are not dealing with someone healthy. You are dealing with a narcissist who is becoming an adult, and you are dealing with a trauma associated with the development of narcissus, which can even go into adulthood. His feelings for a narcissistic brother today have their source in the treatment he received when he was younger. For example, if you feel anxiety around you, this is because part of you is waiting for an attack. Past injuries still exist, and when you meet a rapist, you experience a fight-like or flight-like response, even if there is no immediate threat. Also, if his brutal brother treats him better, he will always be on his guard. Your new civilization is an act, a way to hide the abuse of the past, but deep down, you'll ever feel that there is still all hostility and aggression lurking beneath the surface.

Dealing with narcissistic siblings or parents

The only thing to remember if he is a narcissistic brother or a father or both is that they are ultimately narcissistic. This means that they are in it for themselves, want, and must-see themselves as their superiors and will do bad things to maintain this illusion. Just who they are and what they are, and you can't change them. On the other hand, you can change it. Remember that all relationships are optional, including family relationships. Of course, you have a biological relationship with a narcissist who threw you out of your birth canal, just like you do with a brother who has made this journey in front of you or after you, but all this is simply a biological accident and does not mean that you have to endure your abuse You can set the parameters of your life that are included and which are not, and with it comes the opportunity to abandon a violent family member. Breaking the bond is not an act of betrayal. You would make a statement, even only for those who remained outside and let the abuses occur and take control of the perpetrator's life. You will be surprised how easy it is to breathe. On your part, this is a self-preservation act. That said, if you feel the need to maintain a relationship, treat your narcissistic brother in the same way as any other narcissist:

Set and apply limits to communicate honestly and unambiguously, preferably in writing. Understand that children's hoax will continue to limit information about you. The less information they have about you, the less they can attack you. Share your relationship by keeping friends and colleagues close together from your narcissistic brother. This denies the narcissist's possibility of poisoning the well if something terrible happens to him. Find out what you owe them nothing, and you don't have to accept or accept anything they need. Remembering that their accusations against you are simple projections of how they look and feel about themselves.

Now that we have a basic understanding of narcissistic features and their social interactions on a large scale. Let's take a closer look at how the relationship between a narcissist and an unsuspecting victim develops. We will return to our example with Mark and Claire. At the beginning of a romantic relationship with a narcissist, part of the plan is that Mark will make Claire feel that he has found the usual charming prince. It will be everything for her and fill her with love and affection. It gives you everything you need emotionally, and everything will look perfect for a while. Remember what they say: if it sounds too good to be true, it usually is. This initial phase of the "honeymoon" is essentially a hook designed so that Claire wants her constant attachment. It gives you everything you desire sexually and will be everything you need in every other way. Mark will be like a drug and soon get addicted, even before he realizes it. Even the most respected, strong, morally aware, and intelligent people remain people with desires. Narcissistic experts will come under the skin and learn their deepest desires to catch claws. When this happens, you are at your mercy, unless you pick up the signals and run as fast as you can in the opposite direction! Unfortunately, Claire does not see a trace of narcissism because she has never met a narcissist who tries to manipulate her. He was never surrounded by people who were not kind and compassionate like her. He loves the fact that Mark has shown his sensitive side and makes him feel that he helps him overcome the pain by giving him the feeling that he gives as much as he receives. But over time, it will slowly disappear and become apparent as if it were not the case. An excessively lenient boy will become something else, but at this point, Claire is madly in love with Mark, and, worse, trusts him. Start using emotional and psychological games that work to destroy your self-esteem and confidence gradually. He will present faults and problems to his friends and family and encourage discussion between Claire and the people he loves and values. It will help slowly isolate her from the people she once trusted, relying more and more on Mark, trusting what she says. Otherwise, she will give her what she needs until she does. Emotional games will gradually tear Claire until it becomes only a shadow of the former self. It is possible that the narcissus has already used gaslighting techniques or is now beginning to present them, focusing on things that he perceives as defects in character, body, or personality. Sometimes you will have a vision of the brand you know when they met, and it will last for another period. But gradually, you will begin to understand that things are not what they seem. One of the first things victims could see in their situation is that the narcissus will neglect consistency and repetition because they don't care what others think or feel accordingly. Mark will not necessarily judge how her public behavior is reflected in Claire, and he can openly show himself, show off, and even flirt with other women right in front of her. When he begins to confront him with this behavior, he will easily deny him and say that he is inventing things, which is another sign of gas ignition. How far the victim goes depends on the victim. Some people have been associated for years. After all, the narcissus will disappear and then appear sporadically, telling the victim that he is unsure of things and that he feels uncertain about their relationship, perhaps indicating the things that the victim did wrong in the relationship that inflicts him. Narcissus's commitment at this point will use everything to cause pain and make the victim feel that he must compensate for what he has done. In the end, the game will end anyways. Mark will be bored, Claire, and decided to move on. But often, narcissus does not allow him to leave for a long time, even if they spend long periods between his reappearance. Depending on the strength with which their chains connect with the victims, the victims will wait, wait, and pray until the next time they see their narcissistic companions. Pain and emotional control are so deep that they do not feel that they can live differently. When we think of women in relationships with physical violence, many people think that it's too easy to judge women, suggesting that they have to leave, they have to leave ... The fact is they haven't experienced this kind of emotional abuse. And the manipulations carried out by a brutal couple cannot understand how much a human can distort the reality of another human being. Victims of violence often mention how they denied or were so convinced that they were a problem in a relationship that they tolerated bullying and blamed themselves for what happened. It's a sad but true reality. Never judge a victim of abuse until you know what you are talking about. And even then, we all have to realize that each of us is unique and that we all have different constitutions, strengths, and weaknesses. How many times have you heard about this from someone who has never thought that it would be stupid enough to fall in love with him, etc.? It is important not to internalize the sense of "stupidity" if you have fallen victim to narcissistic abuse. The fact is that these people do nothing in life except to improve and manipulate others. They are professionals and experts. You are not an idiot for being human and feeling. You just met someone who knows exactly how to use your usual human decency and kindness. After the end of the bullying cycle and finally freed himself from the narcissistic relationship, I hope he will appreciate that he is lucky to have been released. Many sacrifices go to the rest of their lives to die only in misery and isolation, without receiving what they needed and wanted from a romantic partner. What the victim experiences emotionally during narcissistic persecution are tormenting and lasting effects. In the next chapter, we'll talk about the emotional confusion associated with ending a relationship with a narcissist and the effects of this long experience.

You can tell if the person you have a relationship with is a narcissist based on the type of behavior they show during the link. Ideally, you'll want to know if your boyfriend, girlfriend, or even a friend has narcissistic tendencies as soon as possible so that you can break ties with him before he gets too involved in this relationship. Here are ten things a narcissist will always do in a relationship.

I will try to love you

As we have mentioned throughout the book, narcissists can be quite charismatic and fascinating when they want something from you. If you are in a relationship with someone, he will do everything in his power to make you feel special at the beginning, to trust him enough to lose his vigilance. As long as you reach the goal, he wants you to serve; Narcissus will pay particular attention and make you feel at the center of his world. If someone takes you on a pedestal in the early stages of your relationship, you should pay more attention to how they behave to see if they fail.

It will make you feel useless

After an extended stay with a narcissist, you'll notice that when you have any misunderstandings or quarrels, your first instinct is to release him in a way that makes him feel useless. He will criticize you for such a disrespectful tone that will make you feel inhuman. When you disagree with ordinary people, you always have the impression that your opinion is essential, but with a narcissist, it is not. All the things about you that the narcissist said that he liked him when he was charming, somehow become negative attributes, and the narcissus will present himself as "holy" to tolerate these qualities.

Monopolize your conversations

Narcissists are in love with the way people see them, so they'll use it to talk about themselves. Whenever you try to speak, the topic will always change, and suddenly there will be about them. It's never a two-way conversation with a narcissist unless he tries to manipulate you, so he thinks he's worried about you. It will come to a point where he will fight for him to hear his opinion or recognize his feelings. When you start telling a story about something that happened to you at work, you'll never get to the end because the story will begin before you finish your own. If you comment on some topics of conversation, your comments will be ignored, rejected, and even unnecessarily corrected.

Breaches your limits

From the beginning of the relationship, the narcissist begins to show contempt for his limitations. You will notice that this violates your personal space and is unscrupulous to ask you for a favor that he never won. He borrows your personal belongings and even money and doesn't refund them, and when you pray, he'll tell you that he didn't know it was so important to you; The idea is to look bad, insisting on restrictions that most decent people would consider reasonable.

Break the rules

Narcissus breaks the rules he sets for his relationship and other social states without any restrictions. The problem is that sometimes we are initially attracted to those who break the rules because they seem to be "bad guys" or "rebels," but these features are narrative signs of narcissism. A person who violates social norms will undoubtedly break the rules of relationships because relationships are fundamentally social agreements. If someone tries to charm you, but during the first interactions notice that he crosses the lines, gives terrible advice, ignores traffic rules, etc., you can be sure that you are dealing with a narcissist.

I will try to change you

When you're in a relationship with someone, they will charge you a little (often involuntarily). However, when dealing with a narcissist, he will make a deliberate and noticeable effort to change him, and more often, he will not be better. I will try to break you and make you more servant. You will find yourself giving in to concessions until the end; any objective observer can tell you that you are under his control. It will make you lose your sense of identity and eventually become a simple extension. When you leave this relationship, it will be difficult for you to find out who you are as a person, because he would spend the entire duration of the relationship defining and redefining you.

I will show that he is right

Narcissus will show a law throughout most of his union. At first, he may seem generous and caring to lure him, but then he will see his righteousness behind his ugly head. We expect preferential treatment all the time and hope you make it a priority in your life (even before your career or family). There will be a clear distinction between what it offers and what it expects and will want to be the center of its universe.

I will try to isolate you

Any narcissist who wants to control and subordinate you understands that you have a friend and family support system that will not stop you or hurt you. One of the things he will do when he falsifies feelings and gains confidence is that he will try to isolate you. He will urge you not to take anyone every time you pass. He'll come up with lies to open the gap between you and your friends. He will be involved in conflicts between you and your family members so that you will rely much less on them. If you let him get rid of your support system, he'll have a free kingdom, and you won't have a chance against his manipulation.

Expresses a lot of negative emotions

Narcissists trade negative emotions because they want to be in the spotlight. When you're in a relationship with someone, you get nervous when you don't do what you want, when you criticize him a little, or when you don't give him the attention he is looking for. He will use anger, sincere sadness, and other negative emotions to make you feel insecure, attract your attention, or have control over you. If someone you are dating is angry because of small misunderstandings or when you cannot pay attention to it, it means that they have a fragile ego, which is a clear sign that they can be narcissistic.

He will play the guilt

This is perhaps the most common indicator of relations with a narcissist. He will never admit that he has done something wrong and will always find a way to turn everything into your fault. When something does not agree with the plan, he will still indicate the part of it, even if he could do something to change the result of the event. You will never be responsible for anything, and when you take steps to solve a common problem, you will always explain that you owe him.

Regaining control over your life after years of bullying may seem difficult. But thanks to proper counseling and the use of appropriate tools, you can effectively restore power and regain happiness. Yes, you were molested. Yes, you have allowed this narcissist to enter your life for years. It will take a long time to regain control of your life after years of isolation, harassment, and monitoring. These steps will help you keep control of your life and take revenge on a narcissus, as discussed in

Get the negativity of your system

Whether you like it or not, there is a lot of negativity in your system when you part with a narcissist. This toxicity has increased, trying to calm them down and make the relationship work. You tried to understand a narcissist who used you more and more. It is time to release all this darkness and leave a place where life will regain shape. Some of the things you can do to get it harmful are writing a diary, sharing your story with a friend, or even hiring a therapist. Storytelling is beneficial, especially when you are with a listening partner because it helps to sort out your confused thoughts. It also helps him strengthen him because he can finally be honest with himself. Besides, you can participate in mental exercises and bodies such as yoga or dance. This helps to exclude toxicity and clears the mind to adapt to positivity.

Make a list of control events

Experimenting Even if it seems trivial, gathering experiences related to control and abuse helps you understand what you have gone through and appreciate your development: the fact that you will not allow yourself to be in this situation again. Such a memory makes you proud of your courage to leave him and expect a more satisfying life. You realize that you can now live as a free person and cannot afford to return to violence.

Practice listening to yourself

Your inner voice is the best tool you'll have to face in every situation. Shows how you can do things better and never lie. Even during great pain and despair, your inner voice can show you how to find a way out. The main reason narcissus was able to manipulate you is that they acted with your brain's external stimulants, which in turn ruined your internal stimulants, according to Morph, Horvath, and Torchetti (2011). They implemented their selfish motives, controlling the way their brains react to different things. However, listening to the inner voice will help you distinguish the situation, and you can find out when to move forward, stop, or reject what has been said. He will lead you to a new and acquired life in which you are free and understand yourself better. This will help you never fall in love with a toxic person.

Organization of time and space

It's nice to have a clean and orderly space because it gives you enough time to absorb everything that gets in your way. When his area is full of disorder, he feels overwhelmed because he registers in his mind that he has a lot to do. As mentioned earlier, disorganization allows you to organize the space and be alone with the things that are important to you. You will find that your brain will respond positively to life in a clean place. You will feel more stable and energetic to face every new day. Interference also darkens your mind and thought. You can establish a good daily routine in which the most important tasks are assigned to the time of day in which you are usually the most active.

Connect with family and friends

As mentioned, narcissists often isolate their victims from loved ones and friends. They don't understand you anymore, and they may even think you hate them. You have been tried countless times because your attitude towards them has changed. Perhaps some of them are trying to tell you that you do not feel good in your relationship, but you have always denied their feelings, trying to defend your narcissistic partner who has already conditioned you to support them from any form of attack. Because he relied on narcissus for all social needs, it is difficult for him to interact with people. However, the truth is that your loved ones are always happy to connect with you, spend time, and share with you.

Be patient: take your time

The worst mistake you can make is judging yourself and thinking that you are not making quick progress in getting out of the pit and forgetting about your narcissist. You shouldn't be tough for yourself. Instead, you need to understand that treatment takes time to be effective. Besides, everyone needs different periods to do something about it. Depending on the depth of abuse or the duration of the toxic compound, healing may take more or less time. There is no time limit for healing. Remember that your torturer has already separated you from the most valuable people and hobbies. They conditioned you to feel lost and lonely without them. Therefore, healing may take some time, and your task is to be kind to yourself and be patient during treatment. More importantly, don't jump to another relationship right away. It will darken your thinking and deprive you of time to heal. As a result, you will be charged directly to the next report and will not be healthy.

Able to overcome something. Depending on the depth of abuse or the duration of the toxic compound, healing may take more or less time. There is no time limit for healing. Remember that your torturer has already separated you from the most valuable people and hobbies. They conditioned you to feel lost and lonely without them. Therefore, healing may take some time, and your task is to be kind to yourself and be patient during treatment. More importantly, don't jump to another relationship right away. It will darken your thinking and deprive you of time to heal. As a result, you will be charged directly to the next report and will not be healthy.

Recognize what was and forgive yourself

You may feel like striking yourself, letting such a toxic person stay in your life for so long. However, true healing and regaining power involves accepting what has been associated with the highly poisonous person who deliberately hurt him. Accept that you have been cheated and mistreated. Trying to please them and showing that you understand them has prevented you from identifying red flags. What's more, they used their forces against him: he made sure that he had a good job, that he was very organized, open to ideas, and that he was financially stable. You never deserved it and using it was improper. After confirming this, know that it was not your fault and forgive yourself. Forgiveness is now the most important thing. It doesn't matter how much time, energy, well-being, or money you've lost. You must forgive yourself and move forward. It doesn't matter why you stayed so long, and it doesn't matter why you were cheated. It's already happened and then forgives yourself.

Search. Get knowledge: self-inquiry

It is complicated to understand the bullying he suffered and what to do next. For so long, you have only learned to see the world from a rapist's point of view. Now he is confused and wonders where to start. Try to be well informed about emotional well-being. There are many articles and online courses that you have access to that can help you with this. Knowledge is power, and increasing power never goes out of style.

Change your attention

Because he has been bullied for a long time, it's easy to return to his thoughts. These are aspects of cognitive trauma and dissonance and are an obstacle to proper recovery. The reason your mind can press you is that you want to understand certain things and process the emotions associated with them. You should not consider these thoughts of the past but benefit from the present. You can take a step forward and two steps backward. Train your mind to be in the present and future that you have chosen for yourself. To increase motivation for this effort, you need to revive your dreams and let them be beautiful this time. Remember the thoughts and things you wanted for yourself before you pull yourself a narcissist; Think about how much you wanted them and increase your desire to reach them. That's what it means to change the concentration to look into the future and change your status from sacrifice to hero in your life. Although he suffered from pain, after healing, he may be surprised by the self-absorbed, aware, complete, and integrated person he has become.

Regain control of your life, regain your story, understand what you knew, and heal your interior

After doing all these things, it all comes down to taking control of your life. You have already admitted that you have been used and forgiven yourself. This is not enough, and now you need to take the last step to become the pilot of your life. The essence of this is to clear your mind, and thus you must accept that your partner has deliberately hurt you and that he was a toxic person. You also have to admit that you are disappointed because you let them hurt you again and again. You didn't listen to your instincts. They used your human qualities, and they used them against you. The truth is, you had a role in this relationship, whether it's love or empathy. In addition to accepting that they played a part in it, you must also acknowledge the role you played to forgive. At one point in the relationship, I had a feeling in my stomach, but I did not consider any tips that I might have. Maybe because I expected it to work, I love them, or I'm empathetic. Therefore, by identifying yourself with the facts and accepting that this is true, it will be easy to forgive yourself. To heal your inner being, you must eliminate all historical suffering. You want lasting results. In doing so, it is necessary to eradicate unresolved pain, establish a sense of internal consistency, and restore a deeper connection with confidence. Where this is going depends on how far you are going to postpone the pain of the past. Know that this is the right path to recovery, and while it may take longer than expected, with self-commitment and perseverance, you will eventually succeed.

Regret it properly

Even though her relationship with the narcissist turned into violence, she probably still developed true and strong feelings for her. You loved her, or rather her idea, which you originally introduced her to you when you experienced the phase of love bombardment when it reflected the desires of your heart. You fell in love with the idea that was quickly erased by the narcissus left behind, looking at you with the face of the person you loved as if suddenly this loved one has become possessed. You deserve the opportunity to mourn this relationship. Even if the person you loved was never a real person, he was real to you, and therefore you must allow yourself to cry. If it weren't for the loser, I would cry for the lack of relationship he deserved when he fell in love with narcissus. Pain includes five stages that occur, although they may not be linear. Pain also comes and goes, and even if one day you feel better, you will suddenly be surprised when you realize that you still miss the narcissist. This is normal, and pain is one of those things that never disappear entirely; you will learn to live with it. The first stage of illness is denial. You tell yourself that a relationship doesn't have to end.

You can try to convince yourself that what happened in your relationship does not guarantee a break. This is to protect against the pain you will feel when you officially finish. So go through anger. At this point, recognize the truth in front of you: the narcissus was violent. At this point, you realize the narcissus for who she is, and it annoys you. The mere idea of his abuse or the perpetrator who asked him is enough to enrage him. Third, it's about negotiations. At this point, the anger has weakened a little, and you tell yourself that there are ways or reasons why the relationship may continue to work.

You tell yourself that if you try a little more or do even more, the abuse will never happen again. That's enough to save the relationship, you tell yourself, and try to face it, also if your currency ends in the sense of well-being, such as the decision that you are ready to be a martyr for a narcissist because you love him. In this way, you achieve a state of depression. Here you recognize that the relationship is over. See that things will never be acceptable and that they dissipate the hope you have felt. You finally get acceptance. At this point, even if you disagree with what happened or that your relationship ends, accept the result, and never try to fight it again.

Therapy

Trauma, especially abuse of someone you love and trust, can be very harmful to a person. You may think that sometimes it is difficult for you to do this, or that some of your uncertainties that the narcissus has installed are so deeply rooted that you will never get out of them. You may not have a clear idea of where to go with healing, and you feel you need guidance. Regardless of whether you deal with abuse better or worse than the average, you can take advantage of seeking therapy. Almost everyone in this world would benefit from treatment in some way. Therapy teaches us how to solve problems better, how to deal with negativity, how to think, and sometimes helps develop severe traumatic events. What happened to the narcissist can almost certainly be considered traumatic, and do not hesitate to use therapy if you think it can be helpful. With an authorized professional on your side, you will be gentle and without judgment, guided through the healing process with someone ready to talk to you about what you are experiencing. You will have someone who can give you real and valuable comments on why you think about how you do it or about what makes you do so on your side, keeping your hand while working on healing. This can be valuable, especially if your partner was particularly aggressive or struggling with thoughts of harming yourself, suicide, or feel that your mental health may suffer. If you think that participation in therapy is a good option for you, you should start by asking your family doctor for a referral in your area, or you can search for therapists in your area on the Internet. Do not be discouraged because you think the therapy is stigmatized: there is nothing wrong with taking care of yourself, even if it requires the involvement of a professional. Remember that no one would think twice if you went to the doctor if your ankles broke, and you should not be seen as struggling with mental health. You can do it if you propose it, and you should never let other people make you feel that you are making the wrong decision.

Reports

This is accompanied by personal hygiene, but it is so important that it deserves its category. Affirmations are small phrases that you repeat in moments of weakness or when you think you may be making the wrong decision that will help you stay firm at the moment. When you develop affirmations and use them regularly, you can recite them to help you begin to transform your negative thoughts into much more productive beliefs.

Confirmation consists of three key elements: it must be positive, contemporary, and focused on you. Keeping it in a positive sense means that you are thinking about positive aspects that may be enough to change your attitude towards something. Doing it in the present tense means that you are announcing that it is correct at the moment. Doing it on you gives you control. In the end, you will have control over yourself and only yourself, and remembering what you should do or how you feel in an awkward moment will benefit you. As long as these three criteria are met, everything is fine. Here are some examples of statements for someone who treats narcissistic bullying: merit and respect. I am happy with what I am now and accept myself, along with all my shortcomings. Imperfection is entirely reasonable, and I agree with it. Every day, every hour, I am a step closer to healing and the next step in my journey. It is always worth taking the next level, even in the face of adversity. My perception of reality is accurate and reliable, and I have to trust whatever happens. I'm as good as today, but I should always try to improve by tomorrow.

You need to get away from the narcissist because an extended stay is not suitable for you. There are, however, situations in which a given narcissist is an essential part of his life, and it is entirely impractical to leave altogether. For example, it could be a spouse with whom you have children, a family member, or a classmate. In such cases, you can try to keep the distance between them as close as possible and, at the same time, try to limit the damage done to your children, other family members, or career, respectively. If their lives are not yet entwined, you can break them, leave them, and avoid complete contact. Remember, they don't really care about you, so don't worry too much about how they'll feel when they're done. Don't worry about explaining too many details about why you are leaving. Remember that if you take the time to justify yourself, they will try to dissuade you from doing so. Break into a public place and leave, never come back. Do not accept friendship with them or moving in the future, regardless of their stubbornness. Some psychologists even suggest that I should quit narcissi over the phone because there is no way to know what the meetings will look like in person. When you avoid contact with a narcissist, tell him that you are not welcome in his house and block his number from the phone. If you leave the smaller window open, you'll find a way to return to your life. Don't say a persistent goodbye. Just tell your piece and get out.

There will always be mutual friends who will answer for the narcissus and tell you that you made a mistake by leaving it. These friends may have good intentions, but they certainly do not fully understand how much they suffered under the control of the narcissist. With them, you should clearly say that a narcissus is an ungrateful person, and the cost of increasing it during conversations is that they will lose your friendship. Tell them that you do not want to receive updates on the life of the narcissus, and if they are still talking to him, they should not tell him anything about you. When you leave the narcissus that day, write precisely why you left it. Write in your journal the reasons for your decision and all the reasons why it was terrible for you to be with him. The purpose of this is that when a narcissus crawls into his life and tries to manipulate it, he can check his diary and remember why it is so important that he stay away from him. We talked about gaslighting and how a manipulative narcissist can force him to question his mental health, so having contemporary records of his thoughts and feelings can help him stay loyal. If you can get away from the narcissist, hopefully, he/she will move forward quickly, find someone more agonized, and leave you alone. Since the narcissus has never really worried about you, he will not be obsessed with your relationship, so do not question your decision when you see that he was moving too fast and start worrying that you could end up alone. Being alone is better than being with someone who takes your life.

Ignore the narcissus

Narcissus lives to trigger emotional reactions in people because it gives them a sense of power in their minds. If narcissus makes you lose control of your emotions, it gives you a lot of satisfaction. When a narcissus attacks you verbally, ignoring him can drive you crazy. You must understand that narcissists want attention, so ignoring them hurts them more than anything else. They want to be recognized and approved; that is why they start with conflict. When a narcissus attacks you and destroys your life, your instinct will be to attack him with a reaction of anger and emotion, but if you do, you only play in his hand. At first, it may not seem like it, but you will eventually realize that ignoring a narcissist is much more satisfying than interacting with him, because then, even for external observers, it seems that a wrong person who likes to fight with people and seems there is a mature adult who will overcome everything. Narcissus wants to control you and control you, but you must remember that people cannot take over your power. You have to give it to him. Narcissus can rule you only if you provide him with control. As we have already mentioned, you will lose if you play a narcissistic game, and then it will be able to dominate it. Ignoring the narcissus, you shamelessly refuse to play, and therefore you do not have the opportunity to get close enough to have control over your life. Ignoring the narcissus, it hurts; remember that you do it for yourself and your peace of mind. When choosing to overlook the narcissist, don't worry about the impact of his lack of attention. Focus on doing something useful for you. If, after ignoring the narcissus, he is still obsessed with how he reacts, then he is still under his control and gives him his power.

When you ignore a former narcissist, don't turn around and start harassing him on social media to see if he is unhappy. Now that he has regained control, he must focus on detoxifying the influence of narcissus and train to be more cautious in the future. If the narcissus is someone who is permanently in your life, then ignoring it will be on the list, so you need to be trained to improve yourself. Ignoring a narcissus is more than just avoiding reaction to its teasing. It's about learning how to stop worrying about your opinions and criticisms. The first step is to avoid answering them, even if their comments hurt you, but then you need to work on yourself to get to the point where what they say falls like water. Remember, even if you have no control over what the narcissist says, you have control over the meaning you attach to the things you say or do. When you find out that a person is narcissistic, you should make a conscious effort to stop attributing any meaning or value to your words and actions. Consider them malicious and assume that all your actions against you are incorrectly thought out. That way, they can hurt you less often.

When you ignore a narcissist, you should consider your safety. Some narcissists become aggressive or aggressive when you deny them attention, so be careful not to be with them without the presence of witnesses. Ignoring the narcissist makes him feel like he's out of control, and when you are desperate to regain control, you never know how crazy they will be. In the future, you need to be much more cautious and intelligent, because narcissus will bring his game "A" to regain control of you. Ignore them, and no matter how hard they hit you, don't give up, even a little.

Preparation for leave

Knowing that you cannot change a person with a narcissistic personality disorder, you must prepare to leave the relationship. Here are some things you should do when preparing or shortly after your departure. You will need support to make this happen. Trust a friend or relative who knows you won't trust your narcissistic spouse. You feel lost and only after years of emotional abuse by a narcissist. Trust someone you know whom you can trust. Find ways to regain self-esteem and self-esteem that have been taken away from years of emotional and verbal abuse. Remember your value and avoid offensive and controlling people in the future. Remember, however, that leaving, he can take care of all his friends and will do everything to make him a bad guy. As a person with a narcissistic personality disorder, you cannot be seen as a villain. You need admiration, compassion, and support from friends. Join a support group like Codependents Anonymous with people who understand what happened. They can help you heal.

Set a proximity principle and apply it to yourself and yourself. Some time is treated, and if you have contacts during this time, you open yourself to manipulation to get back to it. You had to regain confidence and self-esteem before you looked at them. It takes years, and its best not to watch it again if possible. Consult a therapist before leaving. You'll need all the support you can get, so first establish this relationship. When you make the final decision to leave, leave! Don't stay. Don't give yourself a chance to manipulate yourself. Take care of yourself. You are dealing with a potentially dangerous person. Many people with a narcissistic personality disorder can be aggressive, angry, and don't know what can happen. If you feel insecure, take steps to protect yourself. When you leave, have family and friends with you. In the worst case, you must inform the authorities that you are moving and ask for their supervision. Beware of revenge. Narcissi are known for seeking revenge and regret. Wait for something and prepare yourself emotionally, but do not let it affect your new life without narcissism. Don't open the door if it arrives after your departure. If possible, keep the principle of no contact for at least a year.

Healing after a relationship with a narcissist

The door closes, and the narcissus has left your life. But not from your spirit. Things that they do and say may be with you for some time, which affects their self-esteem, even if it's not there. It was complicated to escape, and now it will be challenging to stay away and start to heal. The key to staying away and starting treatment is detachment. You must separate yourself from everything you thought you knew about him and everything you felt about him. Let it go Detachment will let go. Step 1: Stop blaming yourself for what went wrong and start blaming narcissus for not being able to love you. See the relationship of who he was and see who he is as a person with a narcissistic personality disorder. Step 2: When you end a relationship, you go through the stages of pain as if someone had died. At this moment, anger appears. You are angry at how he treated you and mad that you have experienced. Step 3: This is your stage. It's about how strong you are now. At this stage, you are thinking about positive thoughts. You feel well from work done. You feel free from the love you once felt for him, and now you can't stand to see him. Spend more time with friends and create a new life. Step 4:

Publish! Success! You are now focusing on yourself and your life. You rarely think about him. You are physically and emotionally free from the narcissist you may meet.

What could happen but it didn't happen

Find out what would happen here if we interpreted a completely different story. The end of the story, we understood was utterly positive. Of course, there would be pain and pain, but you would overcome it. This is not the end of most narcissist relationships. Here are some alternative endings you'll want to avoid. Narcissi find ways to continue cheating on you, even after you end the relationship and leave. Narcissus makes false accusations against you. They accuse you of doing what they did. Charges may also be brought against him. You are not recovering emotionally. You live in depression, lonely, resigned.

People at this stage lose their careers, family, and friends. Substance abuse may be involved. You lose interest in everything. Nothing gives you more hope or fun. You suffer a lot from stress and depression. Too often, we underestimate the toxicity we've lived through all these years, sharing a life with a narcissist. There is a lot of toxicity in your body, and you can kill you. Stress raises cortisol levels and weakens the immune system. Stress can raise blood sugar and blood pressure levels. The result can be a heart attack, cancer, depression, stroke, and digestive disorders. There is also substance abuse and self-healing—Narcissus physical violence. Although most perpetrators of domestic violence do not have a narcissistic personality disorder, under these circumstances, some people with NPD may become victims of domestic violence. That's why we emphasized security in this chapter so much. Stay safe. Stay up to date. Live your life, but don't take unnecessary risks. Unfortunately, some people in this situation are not able to cope with stress, pain, abuse, loss of self-esteem, and feel that they have no purpose or value anymore. They commit suicide. Never underestimate the toxicity associated with a full-fledged narcissus.

Interaction with animals

A close teacher said parents needed to make sure their children had the experience of having pets. Animals teach us about nature, life, death, and responsibility. Animals inspire questions. They let us understand why a hamster eats his children, why a snake tortures his food, or why a domestic cat is still hunting, even if he is not hungry. There are lessons by nature. Owning a pet puts these lessons in the living room, or at least in the courtyard. One of the things to consider when trying to regain control of your thoughts is to imagine what animals are thinking. The best part about this is that it makes us think about thinking. Based on this activity, I could consider such deep questions as asking questions about the nature of thoughts and whether non-human animals perform activities such as what we call thought. Or your thoughts can be as light as wondering why a kitty is looking in a certain direction or what he thinks is under the blanket when we put our hand under it. The second job is to imagine what your animals would say if they could speak English. This activity very well results from the previous one. Now that you have considered the desires and instincts associated with the human concept of thinking, you may be wondering how your kitty (or any other animal) would have expressed if he could speak English. Would you speak in full or partial sentences? What thoughts would you like to convey to your owners? The third occupation is trying to communicate with animals. Again, this activity goes well with previous ones. After thinking about what an animal can think and feel and how it communicates, you should see how you can communicate with your pet. This will allow you to explore the nature of communication and how linguistic it is. Of course, language communication is mostly irrelevant. An exception may be verbal orders for the type of dog "sitting" and "talking." If you have a parrot, the language will be present. Despite these exceptions, you can discover non-linguistic aspects of communication, such as sounds and gestures. Think about how you control the way you communicate with others through every aspect of your existence. The fourth action is to try to understand what kind of interaction the pet of its owner wants and requires. The advantage of this action is a direct examination of the animal's individuality. This discursive activity aims to enable you to ask what your animal desires and expects. Once you think of all the things that this being wants and needs so badly, think about how important this is for the different types of beings in your life. Think about what you do for people in your life. Think about how much effort you put into giving others what they expect from you. Consider how much control you have over this fact. Think about why you do these things for your pet or other people. Think about your choice, whether you are doing something for others. Think about the amount of control that comes to mind in different situations. The fifth step is to give the animal what it says it wants and needs. This seems obvious, but the additional purpose of this is to recognize that you decide to do something for another being. This is not a unique activity. This activity should continue throughout your pet's life. Whenever there is something related to treating your pet, you may think that you decide to do something for your pet because the animal needs or wants something. Recognize control over what you do for others. The sixth step is to consider your pet's quality of life. Many of the activities, as mentioned above, can lead to discussions on the quality of life. It is worth considering what kind of life is worth living. It's a difficult question that people have to answer, but pets can imagine the basic needs of every animal, including humans. Think about what will improve your pet's quality of life. It will make you wonder what qualities you expect and what you expect in your life. To what extent does the quality of your life require controlling some aspects of your life? How far have you lost control of your relationship with the narcissist? What do you need in particular for a refund? How would you improve your quality of life to get it back? Once you've identified these specific examples of things you no longer have control over and you want to regain control over, you can customize these actions to sense that sense of control. In the meantime, if you're still working to find exactly what you need, try the following. They will give you a sense of control and acceptance of what you don't have control over, regardless of who you are associated with. Gardening, like pets and walking, inspires questions about nature. Why do some plants bloom in some soil types? What determines the color of the flower? Why are our tomatoes not as big as grocery tomatoes? Gardening is a way to get to know nature, humiliation by nature, and interaction with nature. One of the activities is playing with potting soil. Children must dig into the ground. See sand, wood chips, and everything a playground has to offer. It's good to know the difference between one type of terrain and another. You can discover fascinating things about the difference between soil types and why some plants bloom on one type of soil, but not on another. Remember that when I was in a relationship with a narcissist, it was like I was planted in the wrong country. You couldn't grow up there. The atmosphere was not good. You didn't get the right nutrients. Narcissus was like an herb that took you without sharing anything or giving away anything. The second task is to look for seeds and think about which type of plant grows best in their position. Again, compare your situation with the importance of certain conditions for the growth of some plants. Recognize that no matter how high the potential of grain, it will not grow under certain weather conditions. His relationship with the narcissist was like a seed planted in a place with bad weather conditions. You couldn't reach your potential when you were there. Of course, the third step is sowing. Touch the ground. Learn to plant something. Mark what you planted. Share your plant's progress with others. Be proud of what you did. Remember that you control everything that is under your control. Check your position, land, water, and everything you decided to hire. You can't control the weather, but you can control where your plant is going. You will learn how much of your environment is under your control after planting. The fourth action is measuring your height. It's amazing to watch evolution. You can afford to watch evolution (changes over time, not Darwin's theory) by recording the growth of your plant. See the difference day by day and week by week. Height measurement. Count the leaves. Take into account the recognition of your participation in development. You have controlled much of their potential to become more of a seed. The fifth step is to pull the weeds. The concept of weeds as a metaphor has already been somehow introduced. The comparison concerned narcissistic abuse you experienced and herbal activity of taking nutrients from other plants. With this comparison, remove weeds from the garden so that the plants you want to grow do not suffer from weed abuse. Whenever you remove weeds, remember that you remove narcissistic plants from the garden so that the plants can grow peacefully. The sixth occupation is the cultivation of individual herbs and learning the healing aspects of some herbs. Surprise yourself with the uses of various herbs. Consider whether everything we need in this world to heal can be cultivated if we only use the resources we have. You can also discover some herbs that will help you relax. Relaxation will help you regenerate. You can also find herbs that heal your body, which will also help you regain your emotions. Body and mind are the best when everyone is well. The seventh step is to observe insects. Leave and dirty your garden. Collect earthworms. Free ladybugs in your rose bushes. Play with bed bugs, also known as rallied surveys. Feel like the ruler of your domain. Find your power and be nice to him. Don't be narcissistic, but fine control over the things that matter to you. Find control in your delicate nature. The eighth step is observing the roots. Whether you plant tubers like potatoes or harvest weeds, the roots are fascinating things to see. Play using the root word. Look at the root with a magnifying glass. Think about what root is and consider the importance of roots in the garden and life. Remember that your roots are more important than any narcissus to which you added your branches. The ninth activity is cleaning. Gardening is a mess, but the organization is the key. Remember to perform the act of maintaining cleanliness in your garden. Your lines organized in the garden will give you a sense of order in life. Think about the correlation between aesthetics and use limitations. Narcissus probably understood aesthetics in his life, but not borders. On the other hand, actively establish aesthetically pleasing borders in your garden, being aware that both are good. The tenth step is to use gardening tools. Using the tools will help you feel in control. Learning how to manage gardening tools is just as useful (or more) as useful as managing all kinds of tools you can imagine. If you can control the objects in your hands, you can control the thoughts in your mind. Maybe gardening and caring for your pet is not enough to regain control you have lost, but this is the beginning. Think about all the things you have control over. You haven't lost control. Narcissus, which you were alone, made you think you had. You understand that activities such as caring for a pet and taking care of the garden remind you of how much control you have. Practice these things often. If you don't like these activities, find something that does the same. Find another way to use the tools. Find another way to see how much life rests in your hands.

Conclusion

Congratulations are all right: you've reached the end of the book! This is a significant first step in recognizing the abuse that a narcissist may have in your life. It took time and effort to question your relationship, and this is the first step in this journey. This is the beginning of the recognition of the bullying he experienced, and such a monumental step must be recognized and celebrated. The first step was to identify daffodils. Do not forget about the most common features and warning signs of a narcissist traveling around the world. Always remember to be aware of the red flags and recognize them at the moment and trust your instincts when you feel that something can be disturbing. You should always trust your instincts because this is often your first warning that something is wrong. Do not forget about the signs of bullying and ways to fight the damage narcissists are trying to do. If you remember to use gray rock and protect yourself as you prepare to leave the storm of narcissistic anger and explosion, or resist it, trying to separate, you'll survive. You survived your situation, and thanks to the tools of this book that will arm you, you can protect yourself. Remember that if you feel physically insecure about your relationship, asking for help is always acceptable. There are domestic violence helplines that can help you locate resources and help if you think this is the best option at the moment. After all, you should try to do the best for you, making sure you are treated. Do not hesitate to ask for help, and do not be ashamed of the narcissist's actions. They do not reflect poorly on you. When browsing during this difficult time, remember that you are healthy. Ending your relationship makes you durable. Seeking help and support to survive makes you durable. You are a warrior, ready to refuse and not accept the abuses that the narcissist tried to use against you. You are not broken, unworthy, useless, or weak. You are strong.

You are a survivor. Remember that you can be afraid of the unknown and what will come in the future. Being afraid of something means recognizing the uncertainty and danger of the path you have chosen, but the real courage is to try to walk yourself. Take a day trip, hour, minute, or even step by step if you need it. If you stumble and fall and make a mistake somewhere along the way, get up, brush your knees, and continue. Accidents and errors happen, and you still deserve to stay. The end of your journey is still waiting for you. Good luck on this road, you deserve the happiness and peace that await you when you finally reach the other side of this long and winding road.